THAT 70s COLORING BOOK

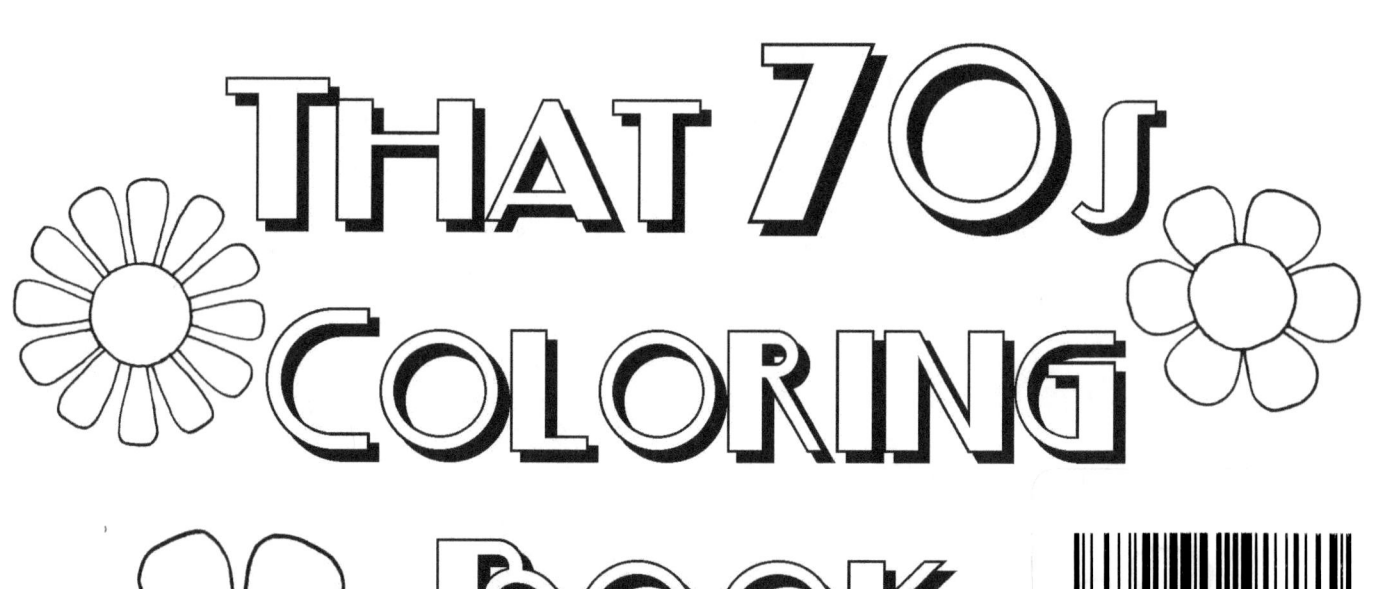

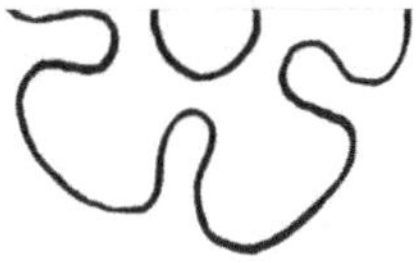

Artist:
Tabitha L. Barnett

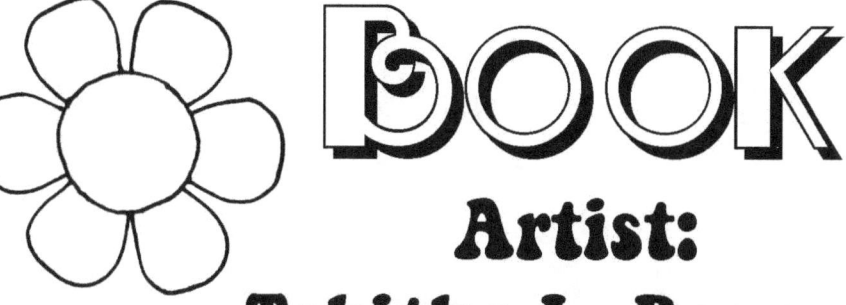

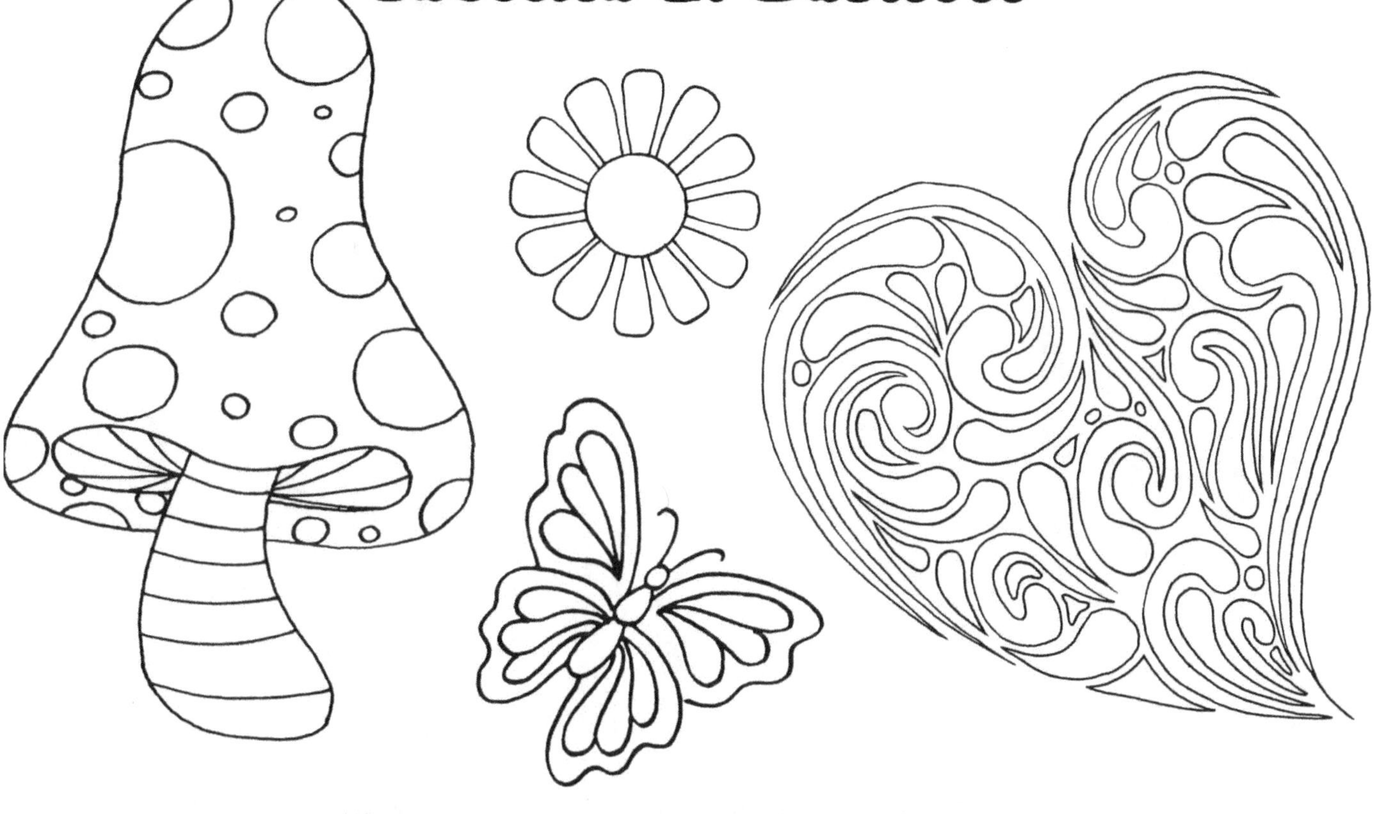

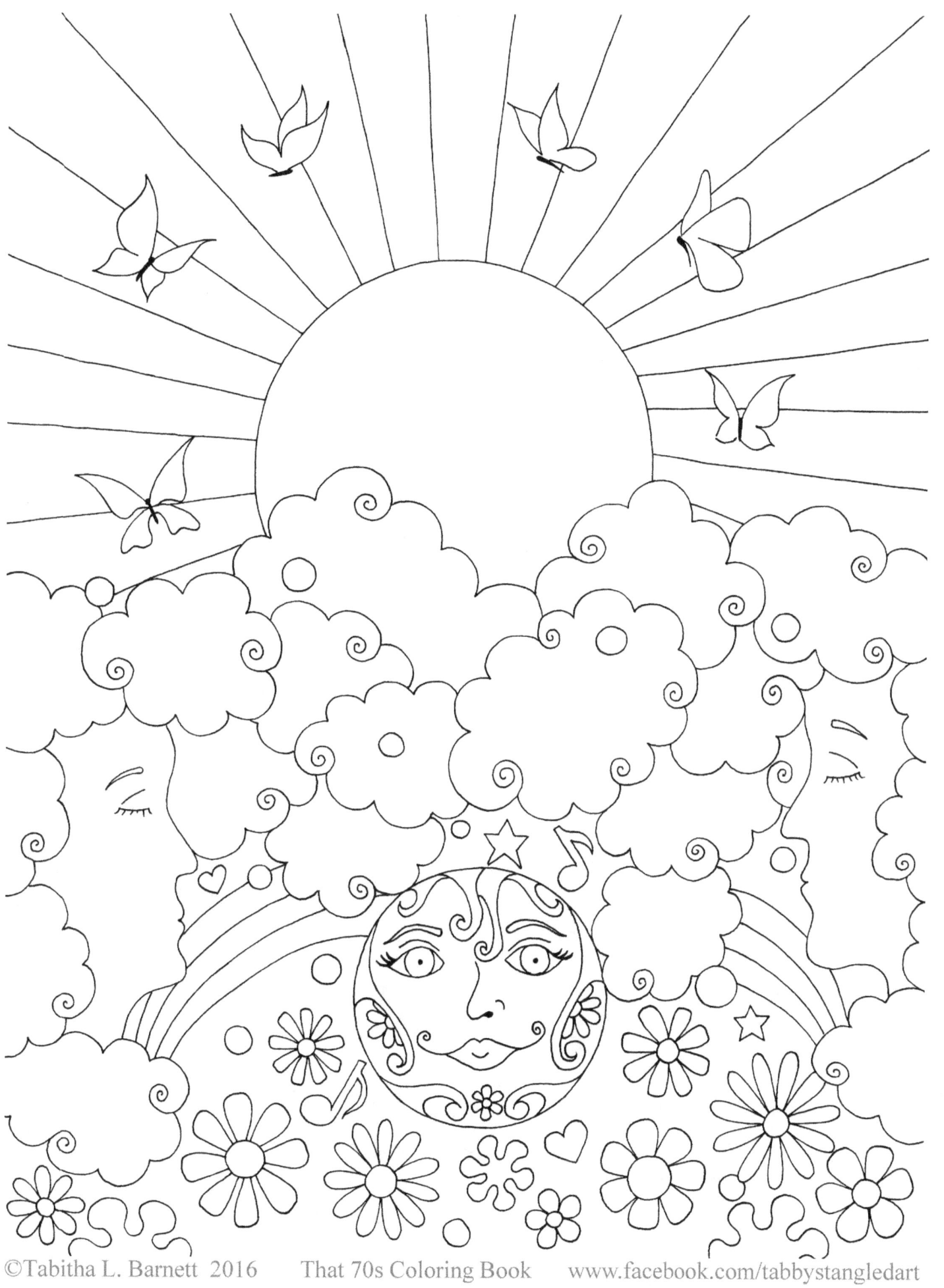

That 70s Coloring Book

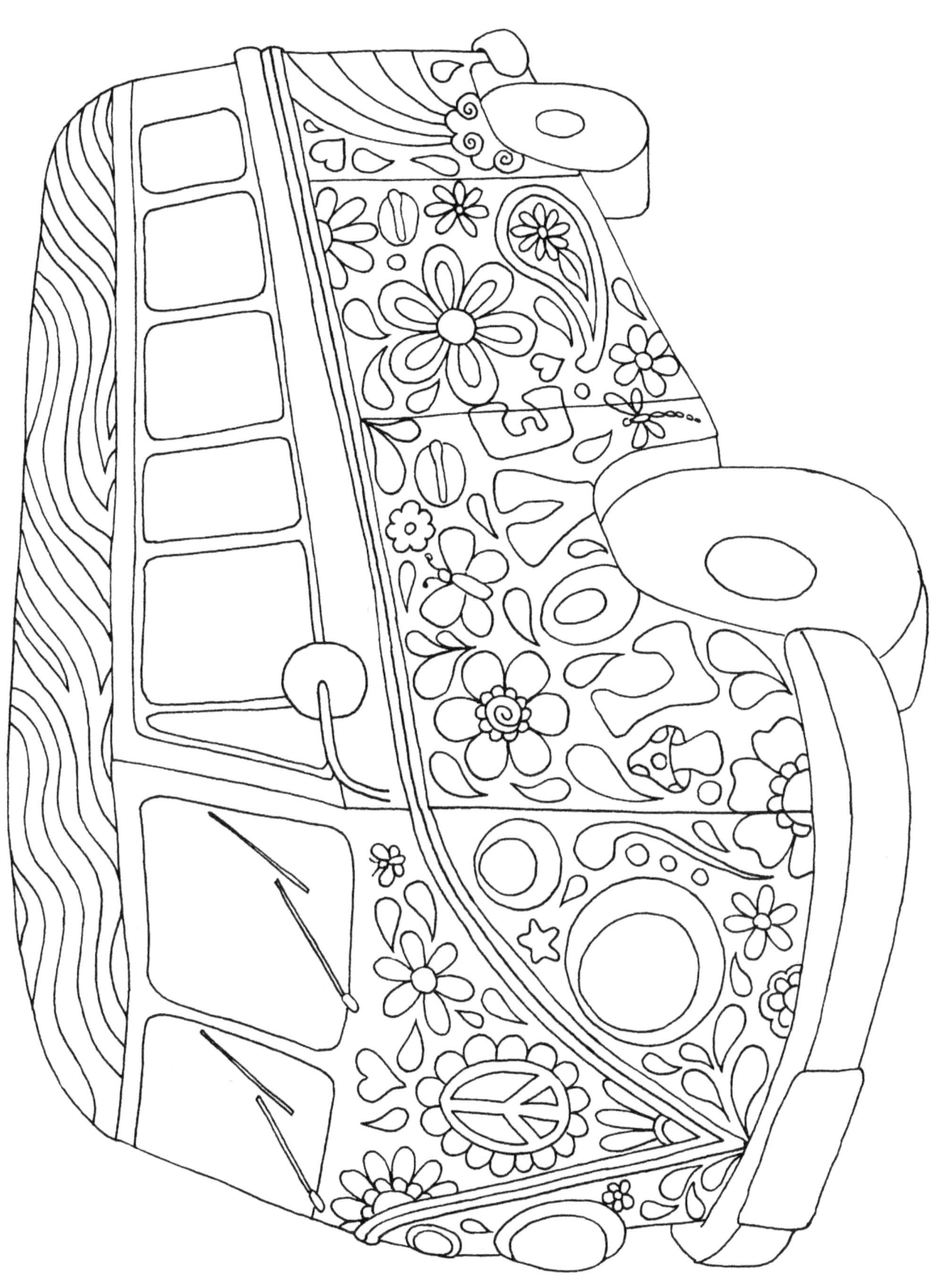

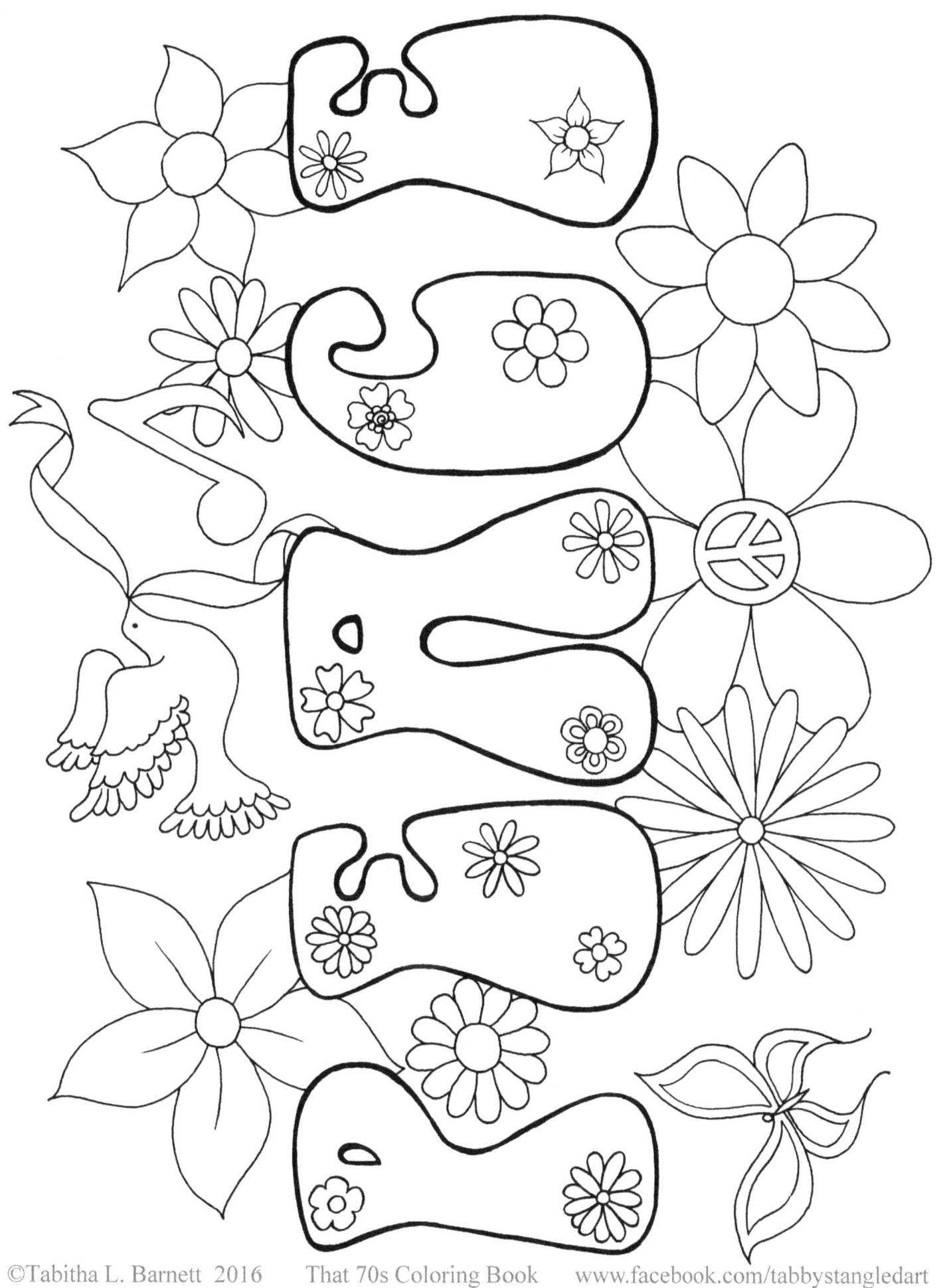

That 70s Coloring Book

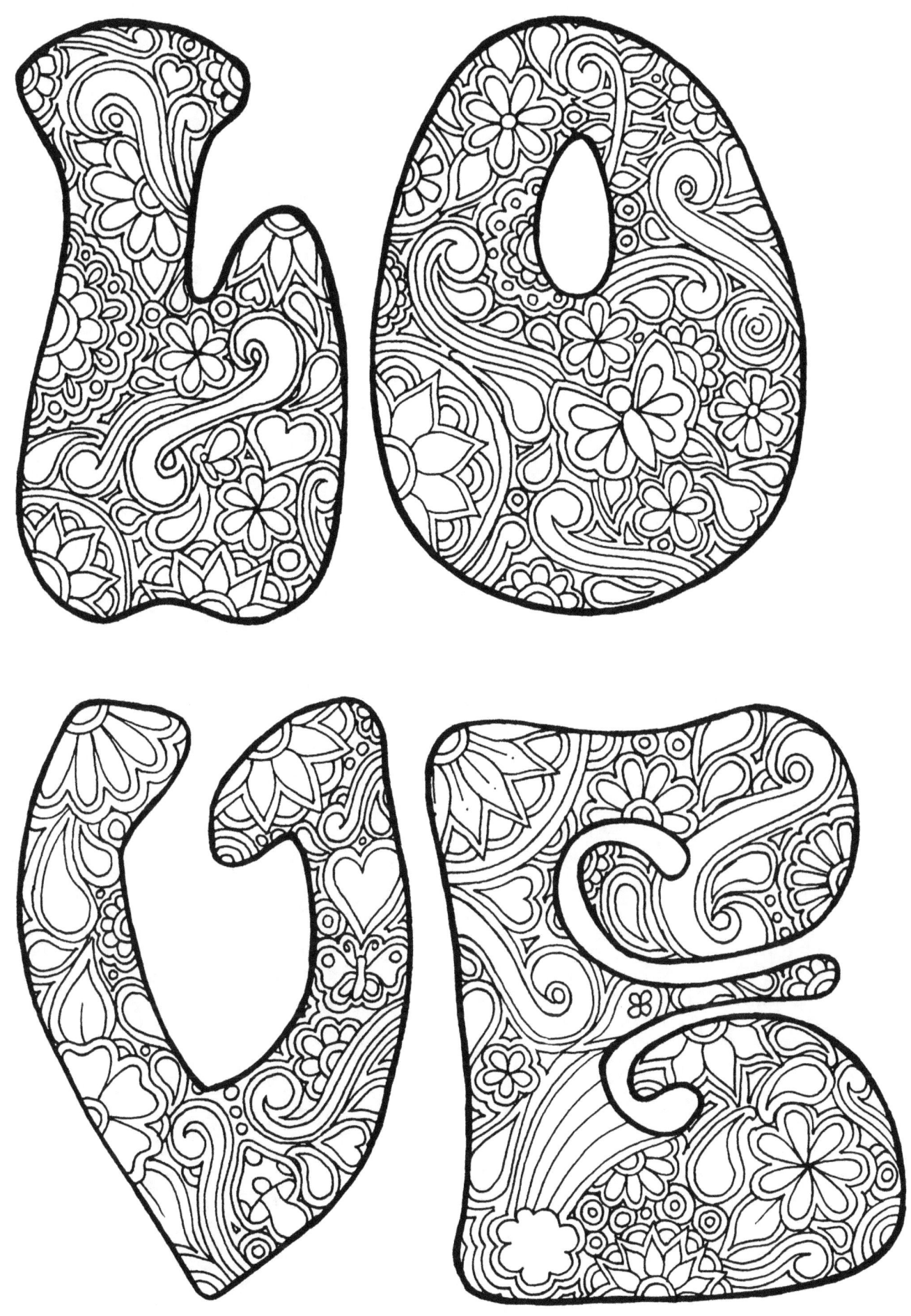

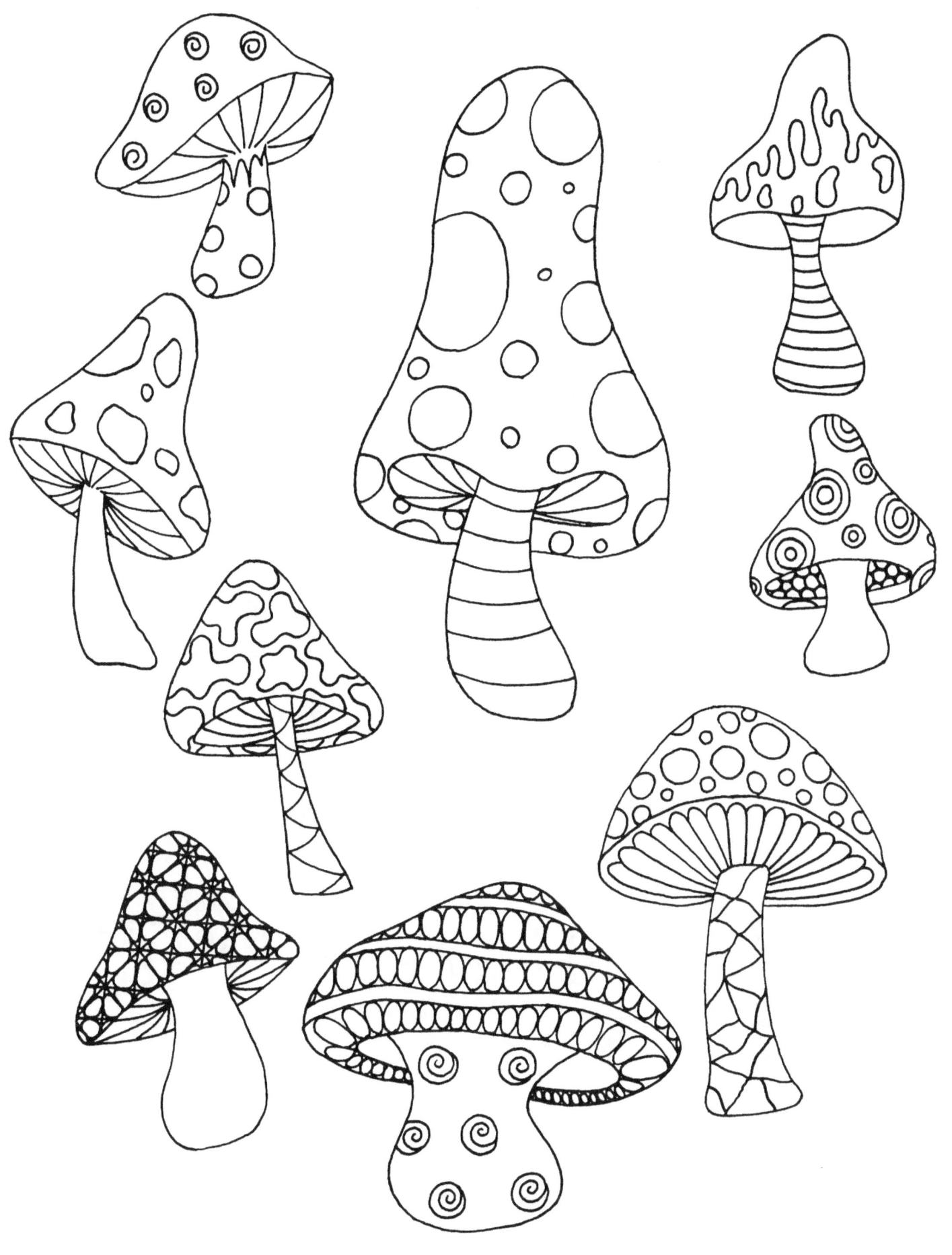

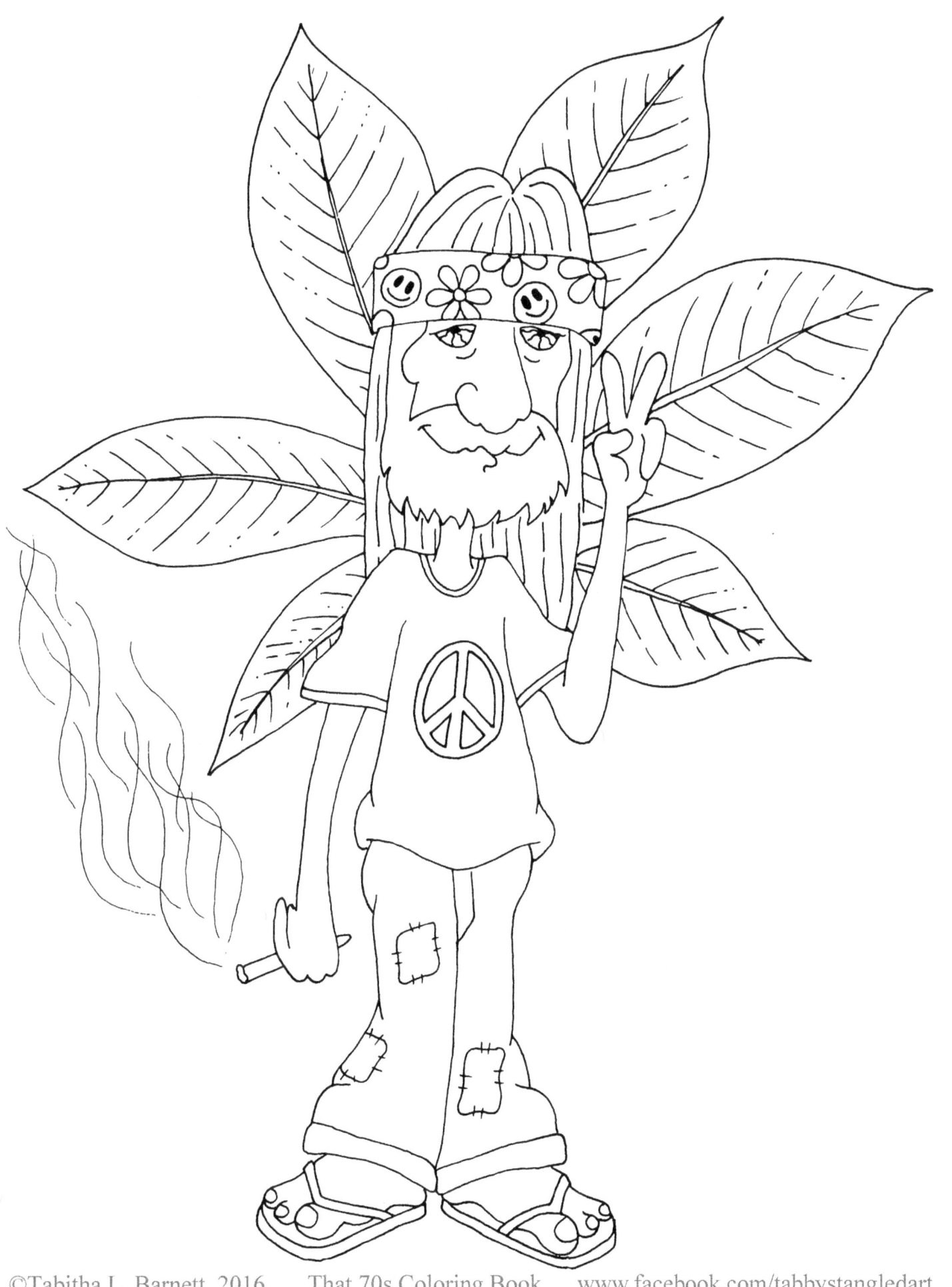

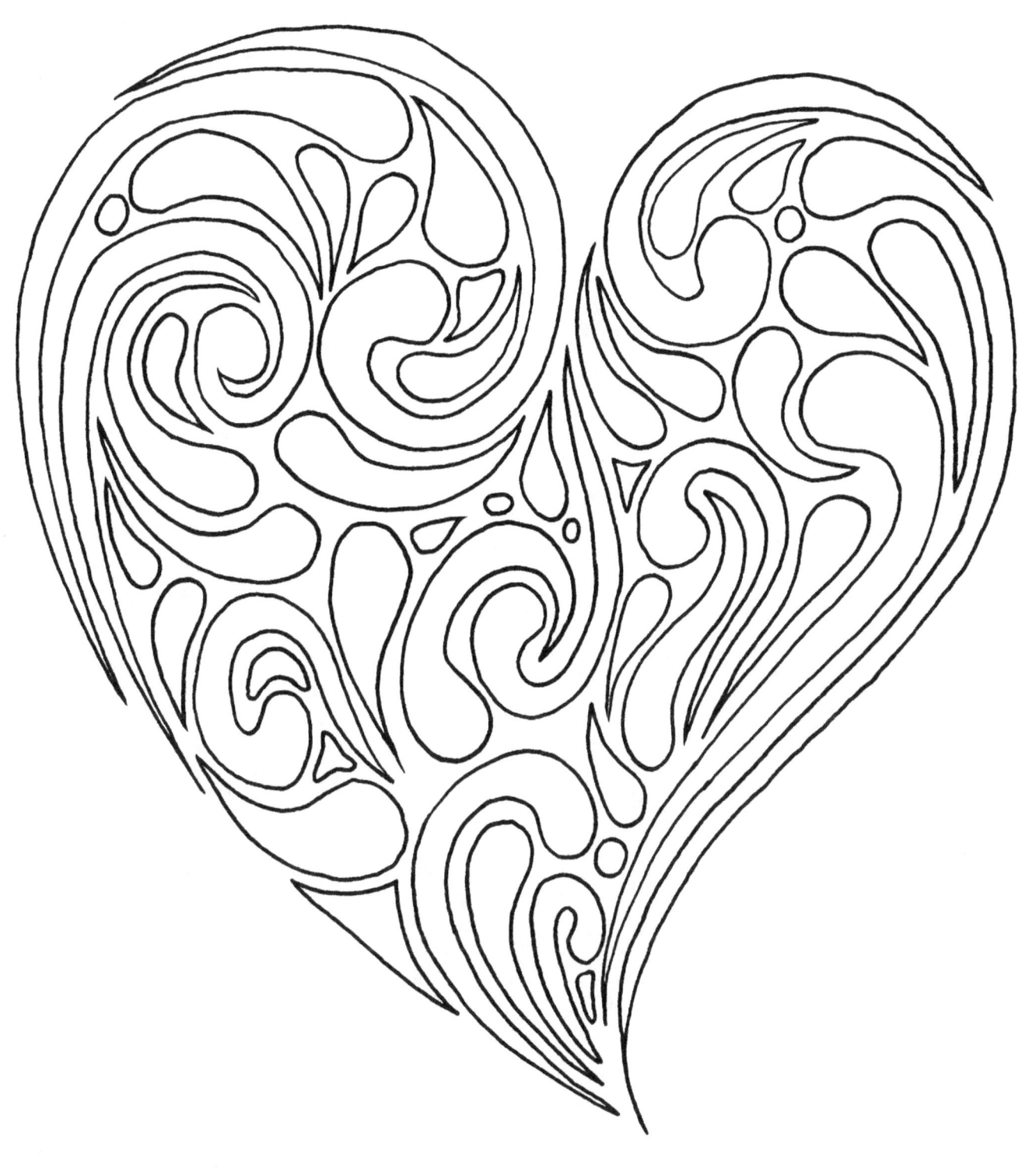

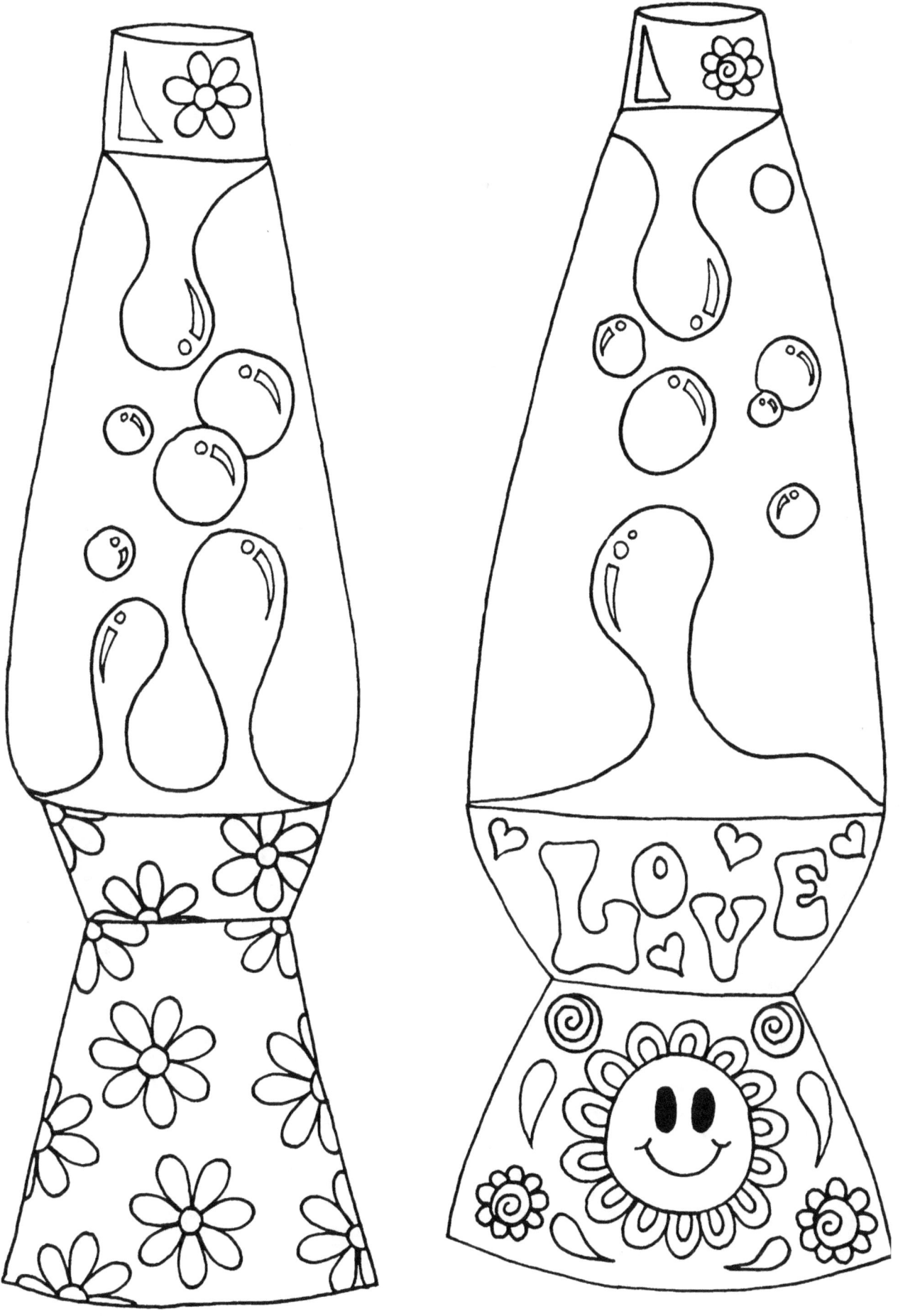

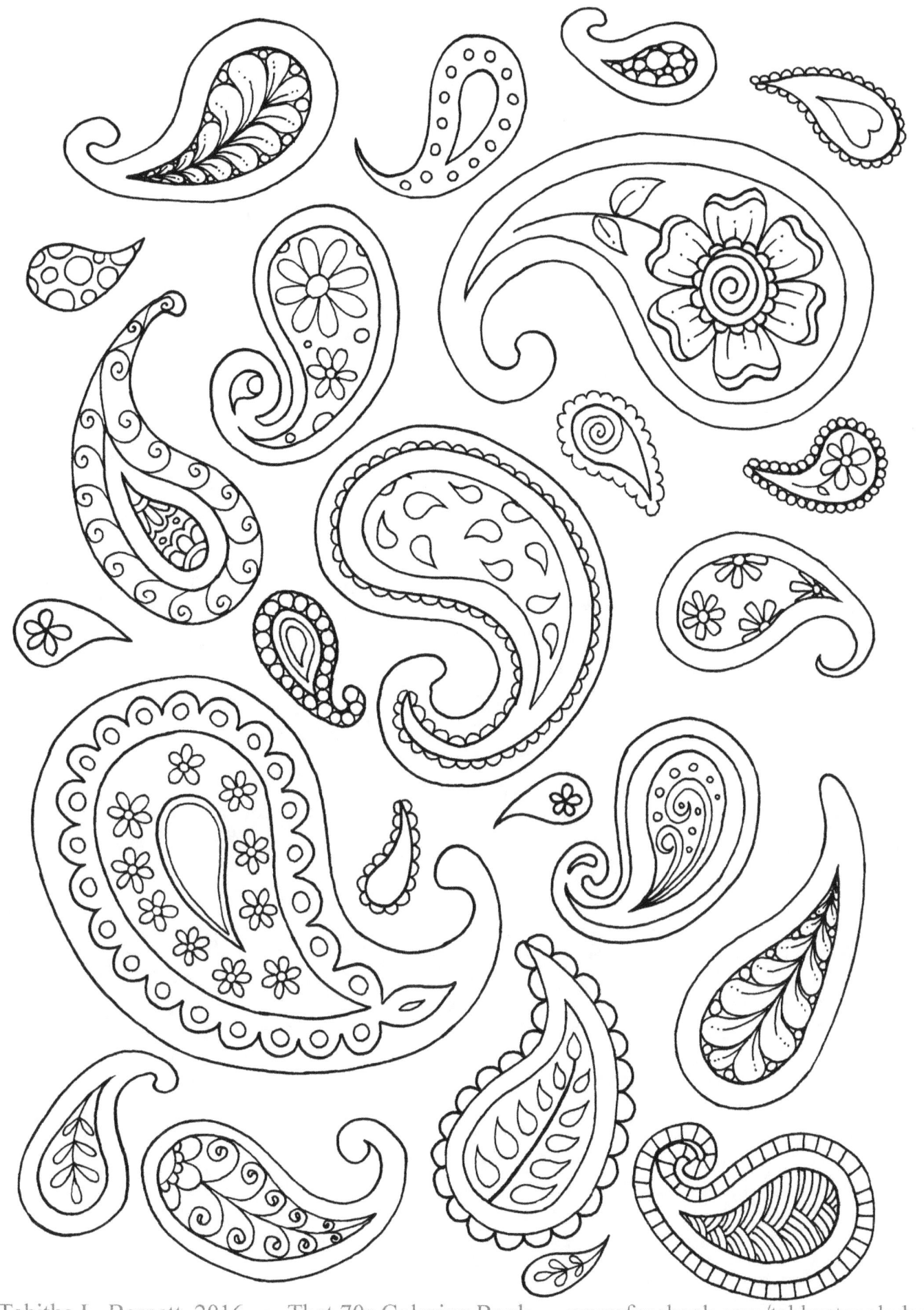

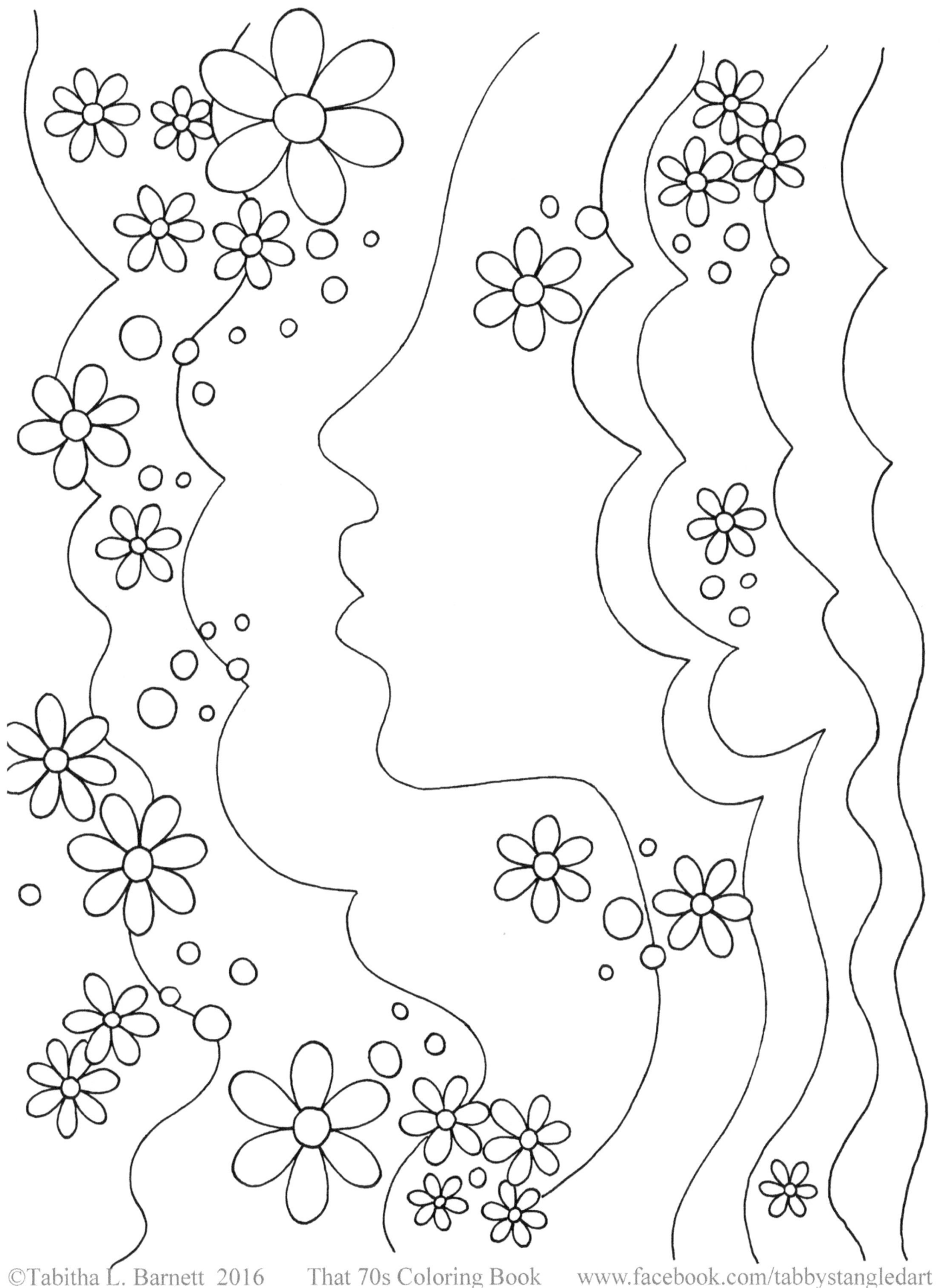

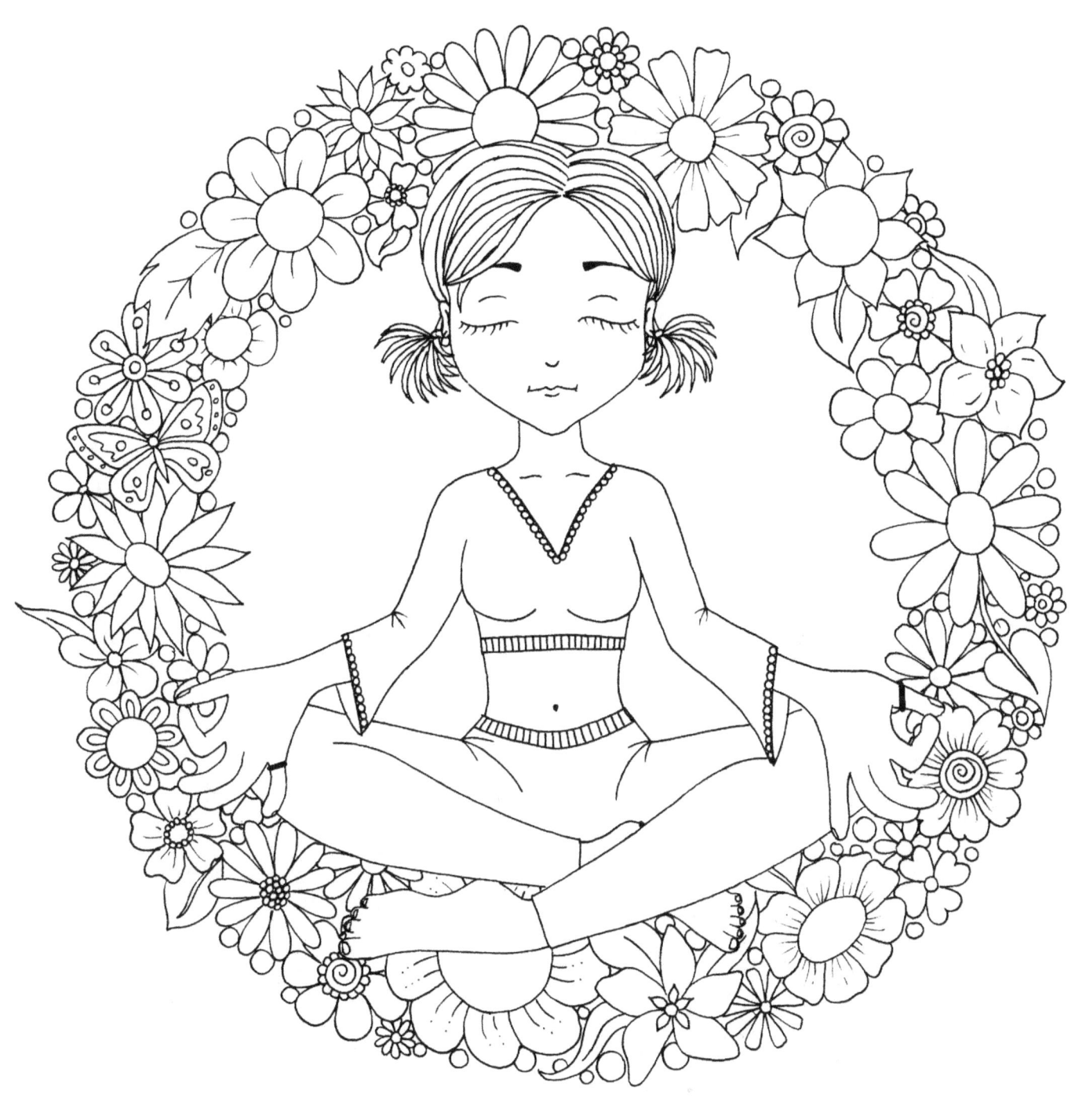

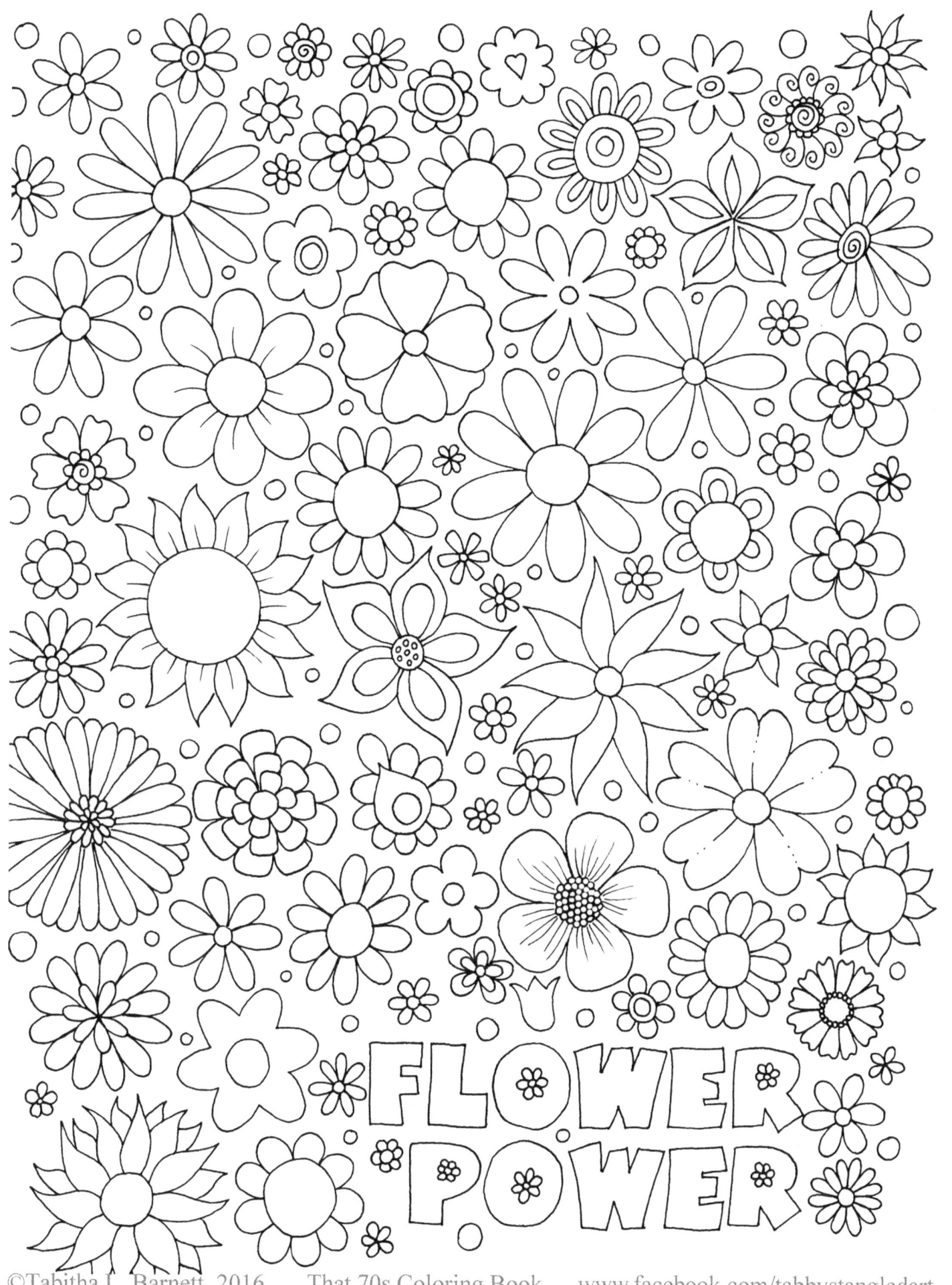

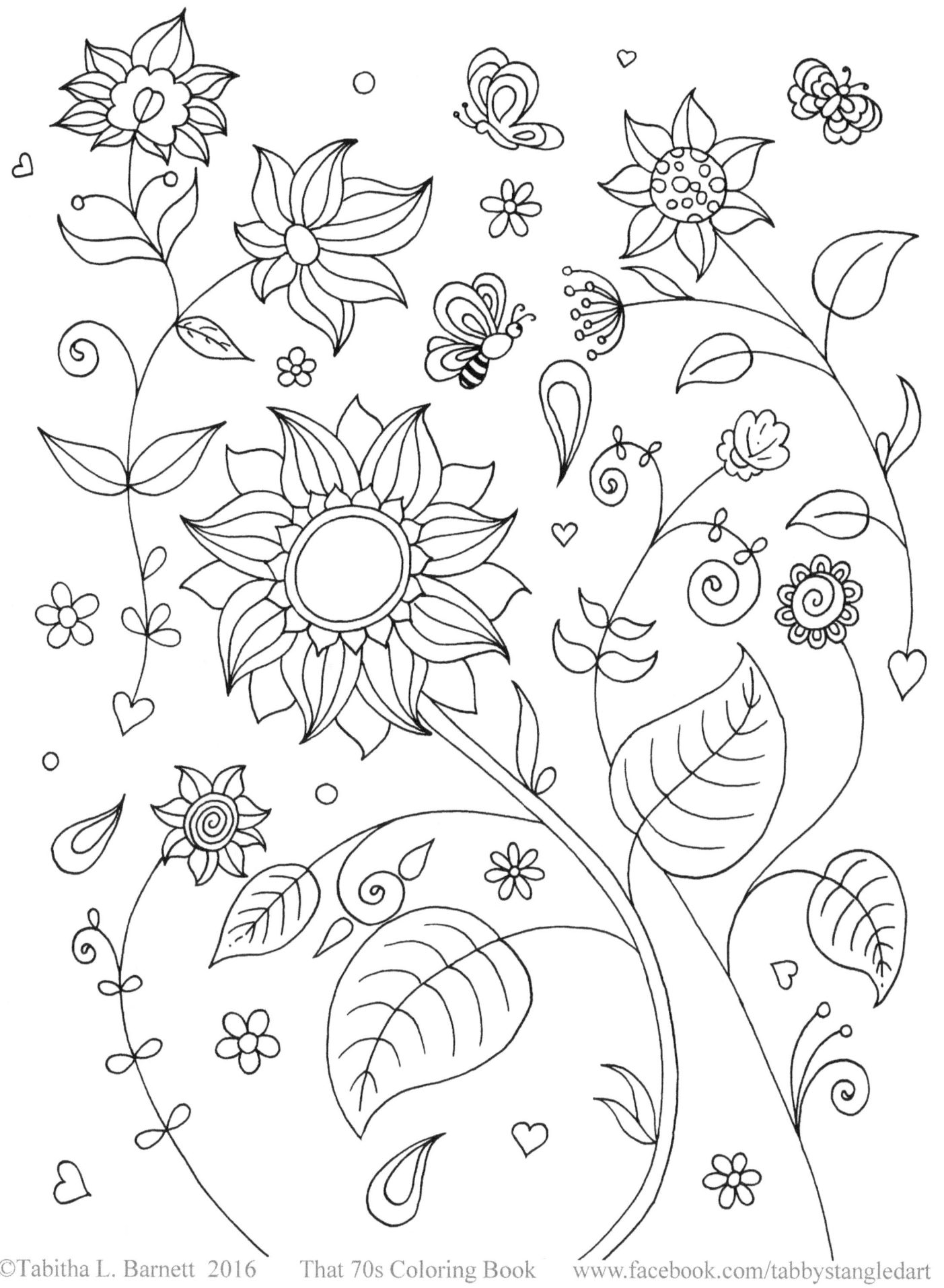

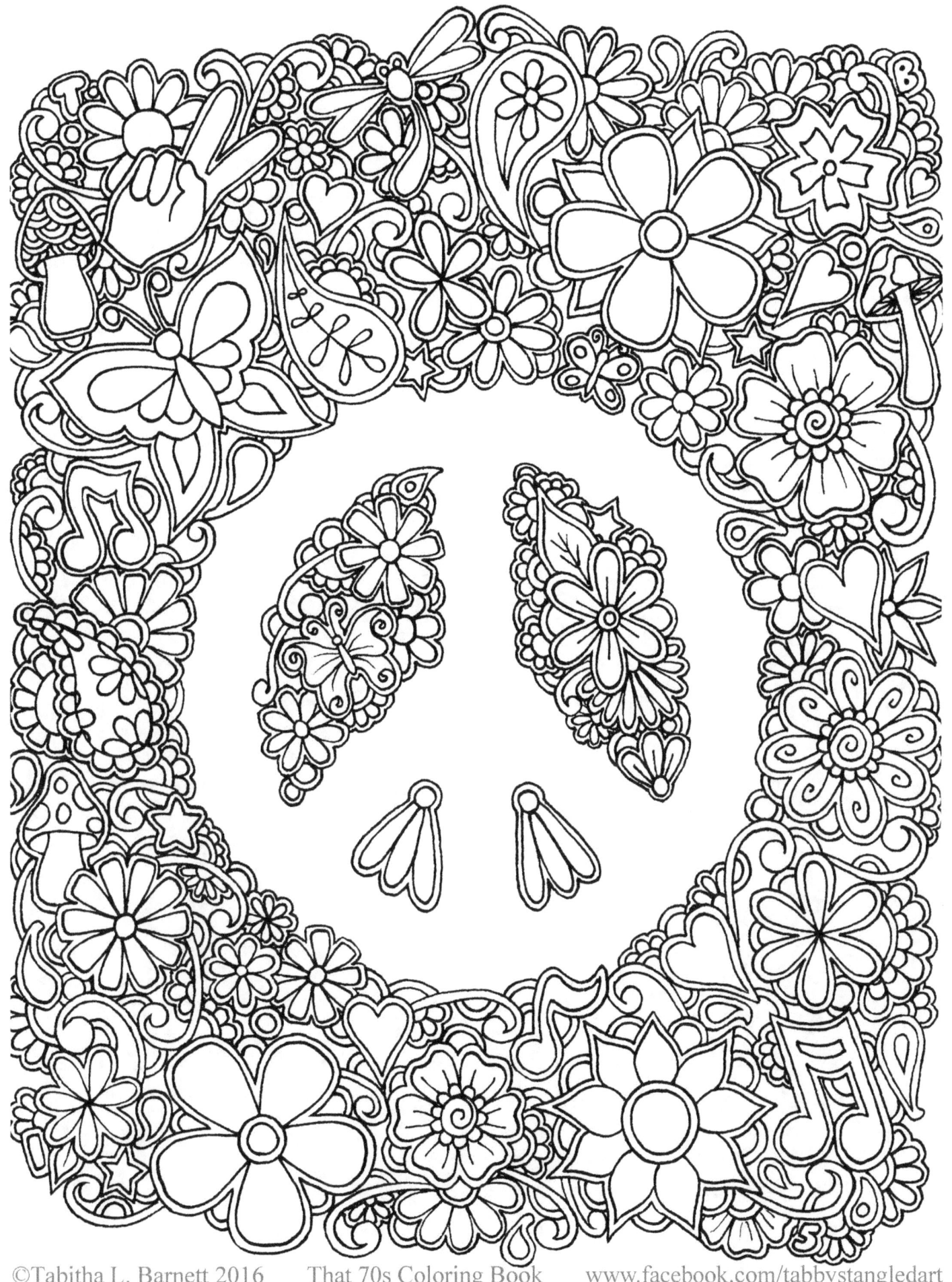

That 70s Coloring Book   www.facebook.com/tabbystangledart

That 70s Coloring Book

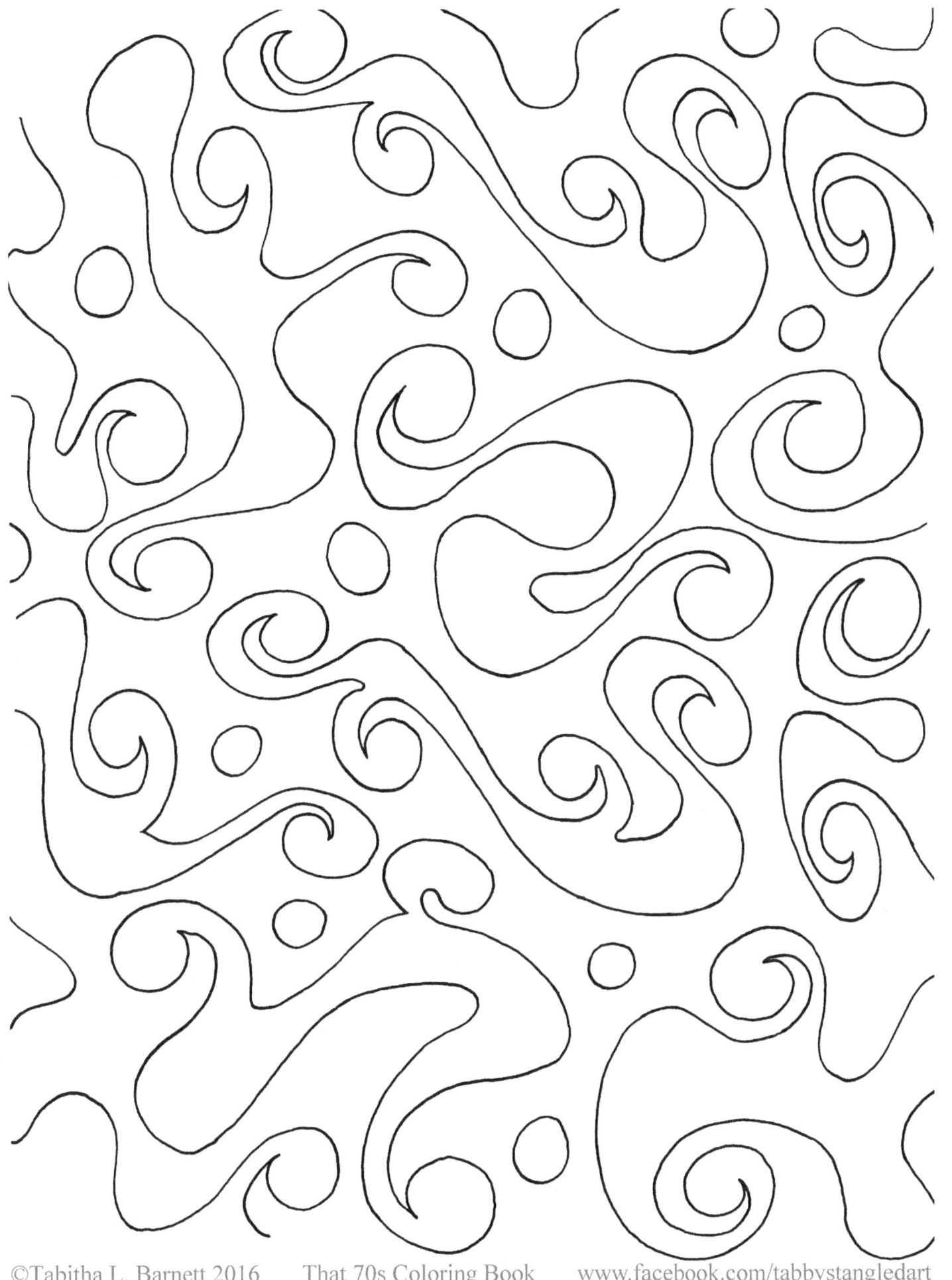

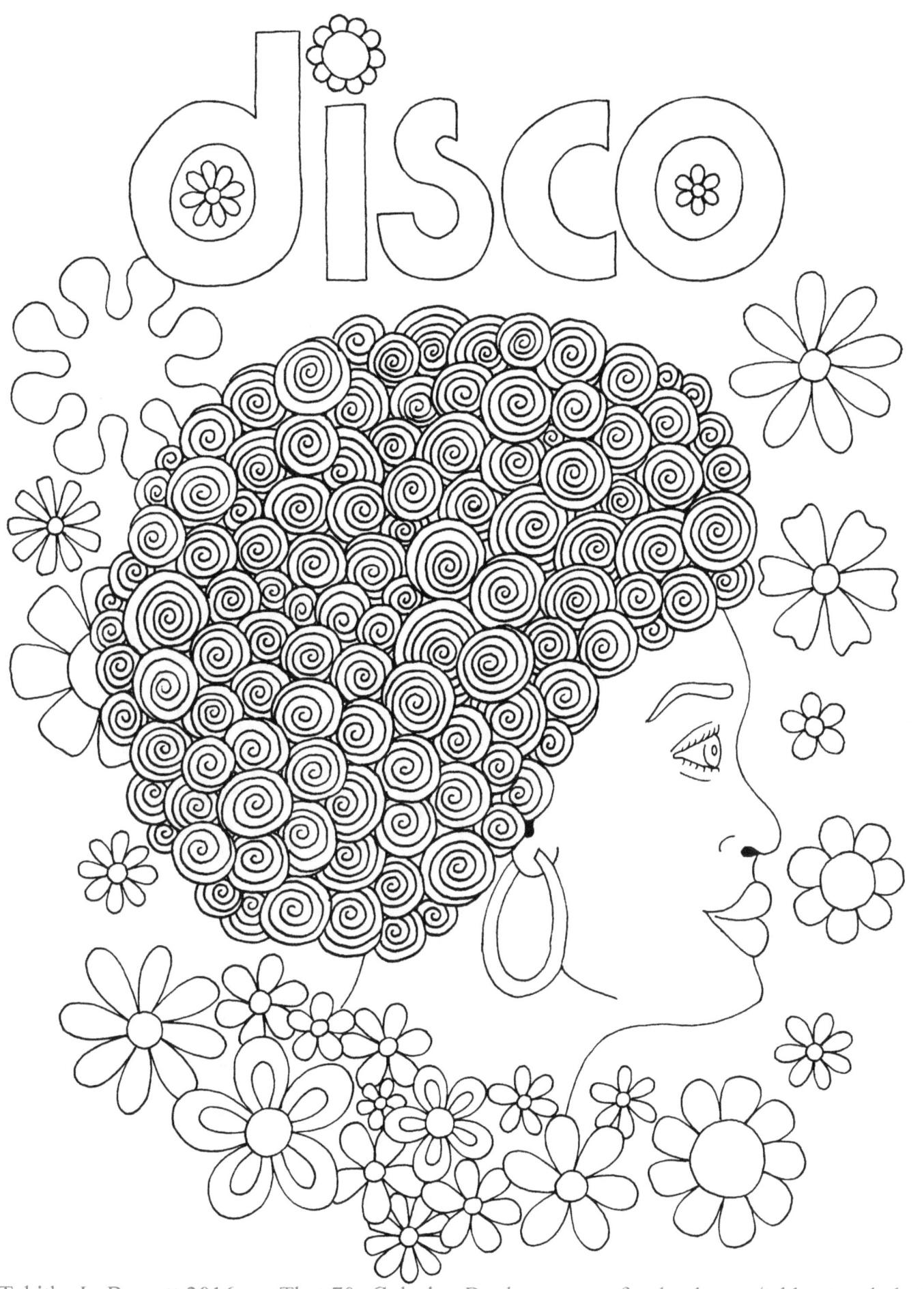

That 70s Coloring Book

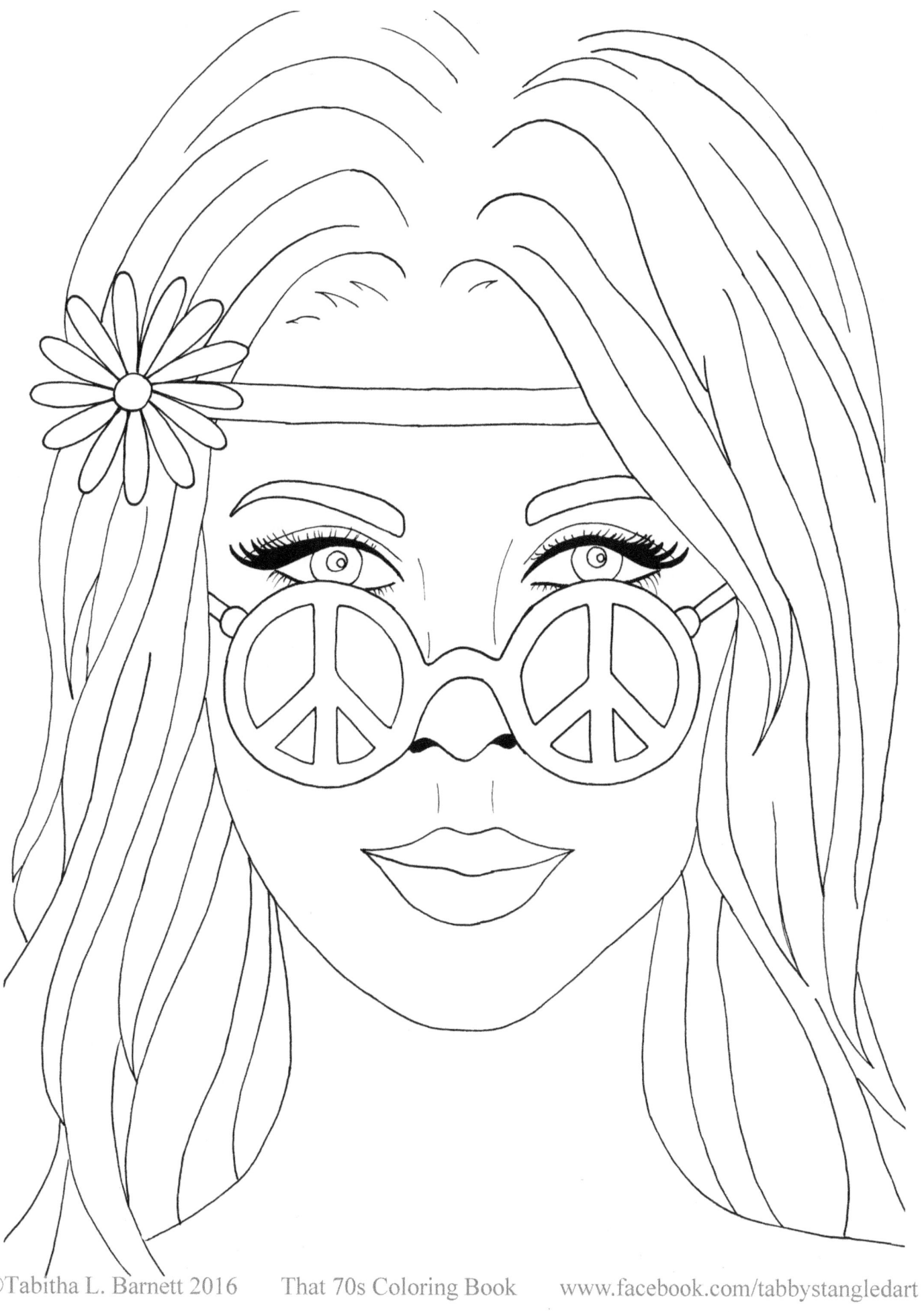

That 70s Coloring Book   www.facebook.com/tabbystangledart

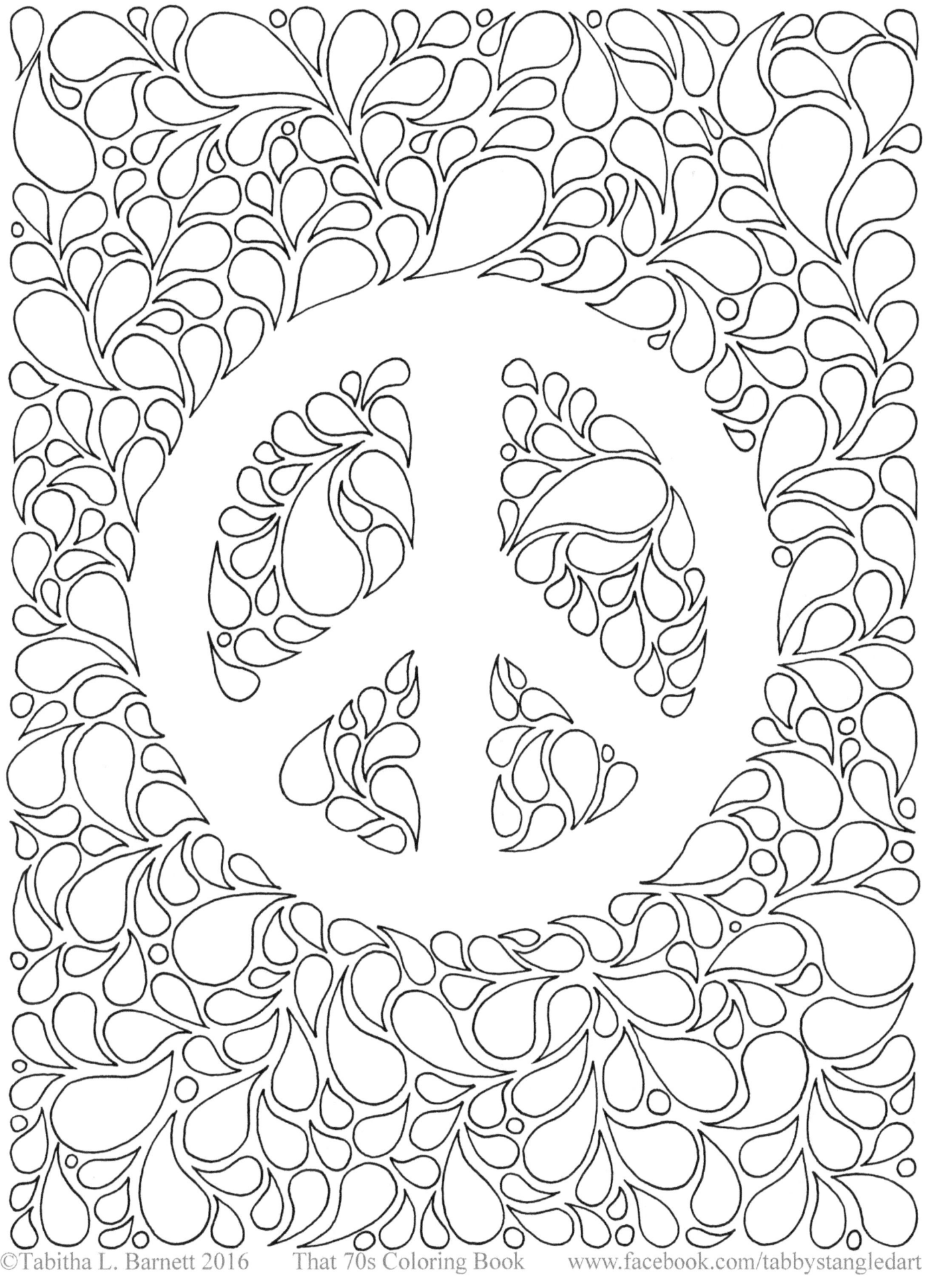

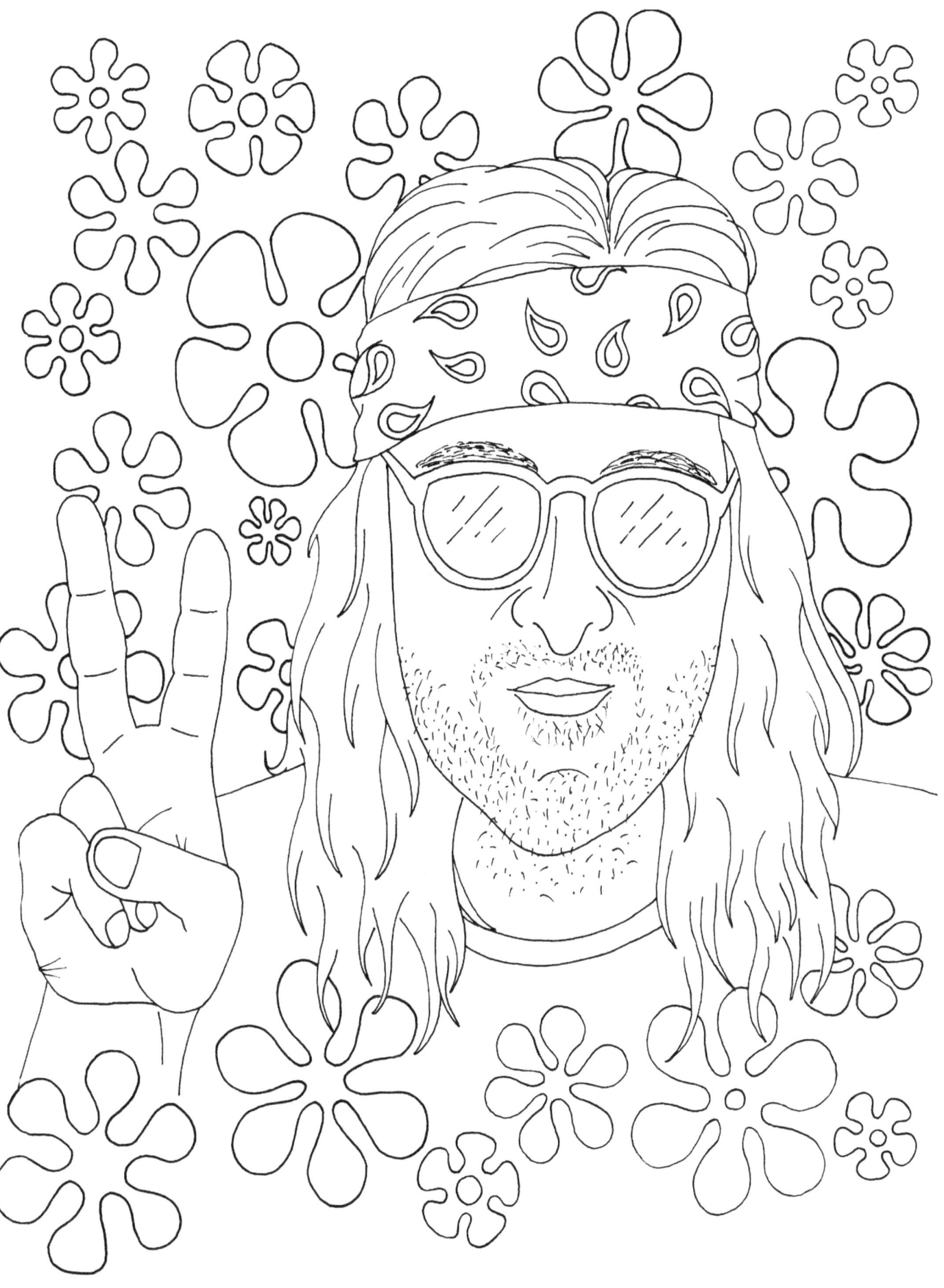

That 70s Coloring Book   www.facebook.com/tabbystangledart

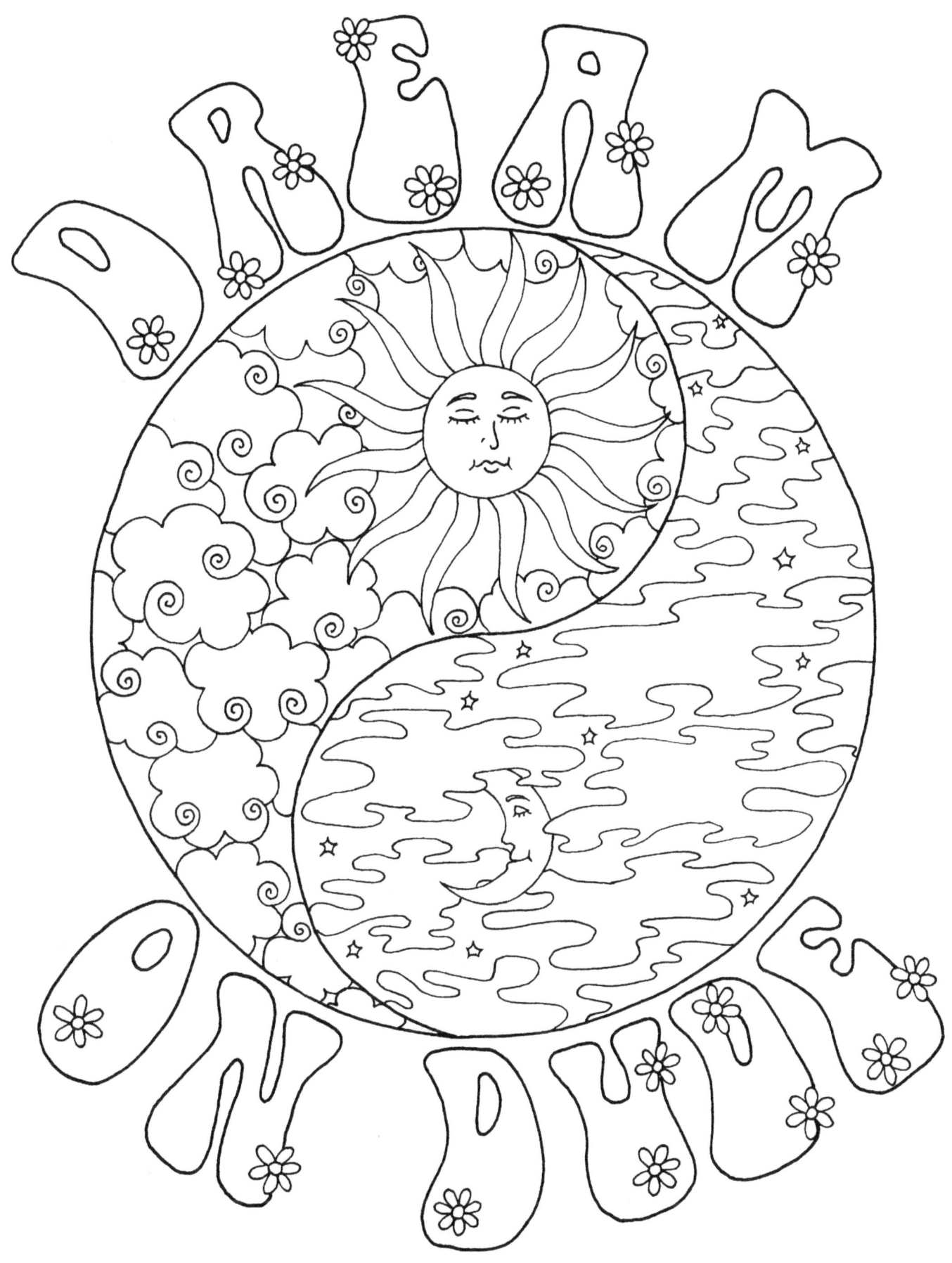

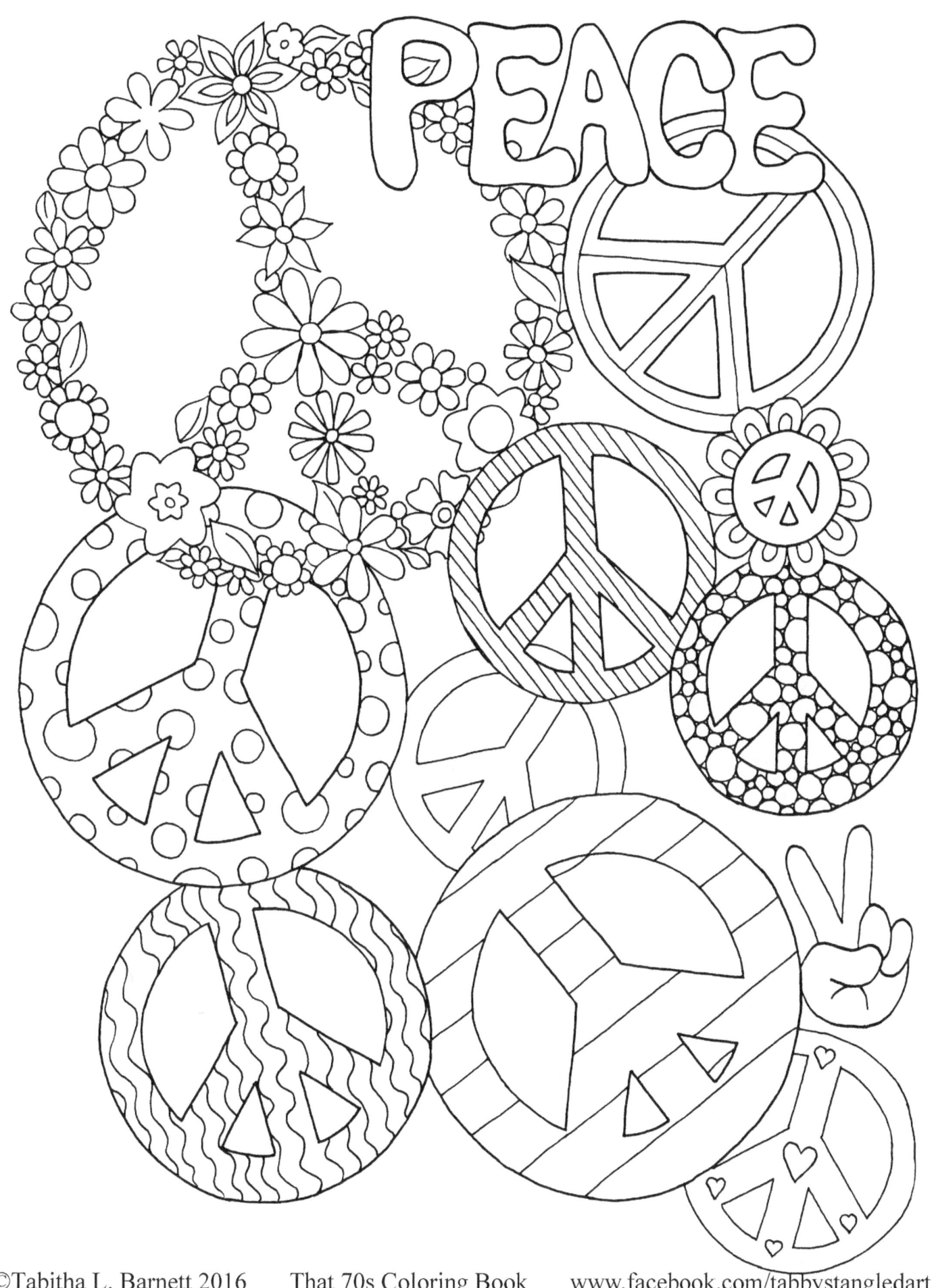

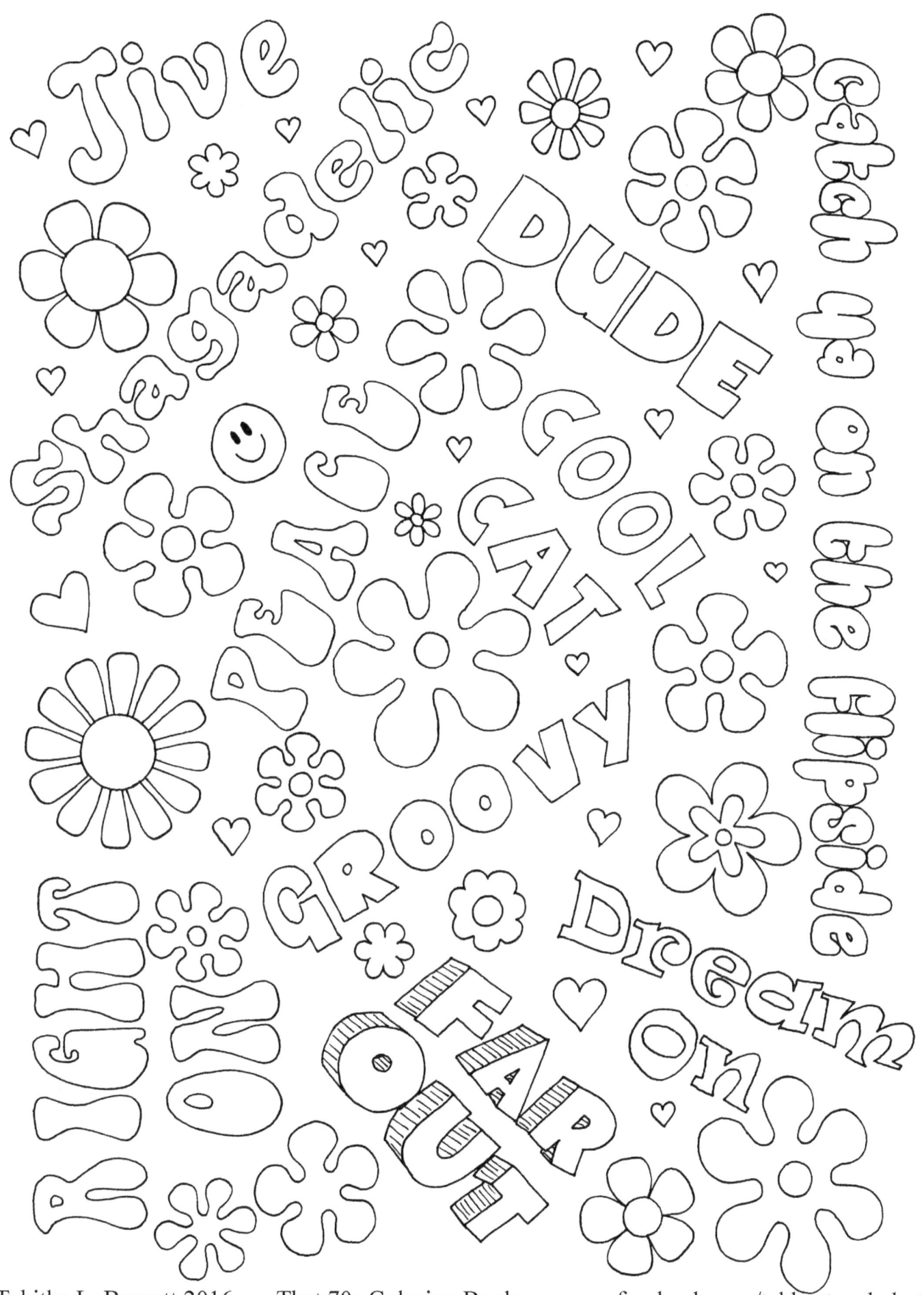

That 70s Coloring Book   www.facebook.com/tabbystangledart

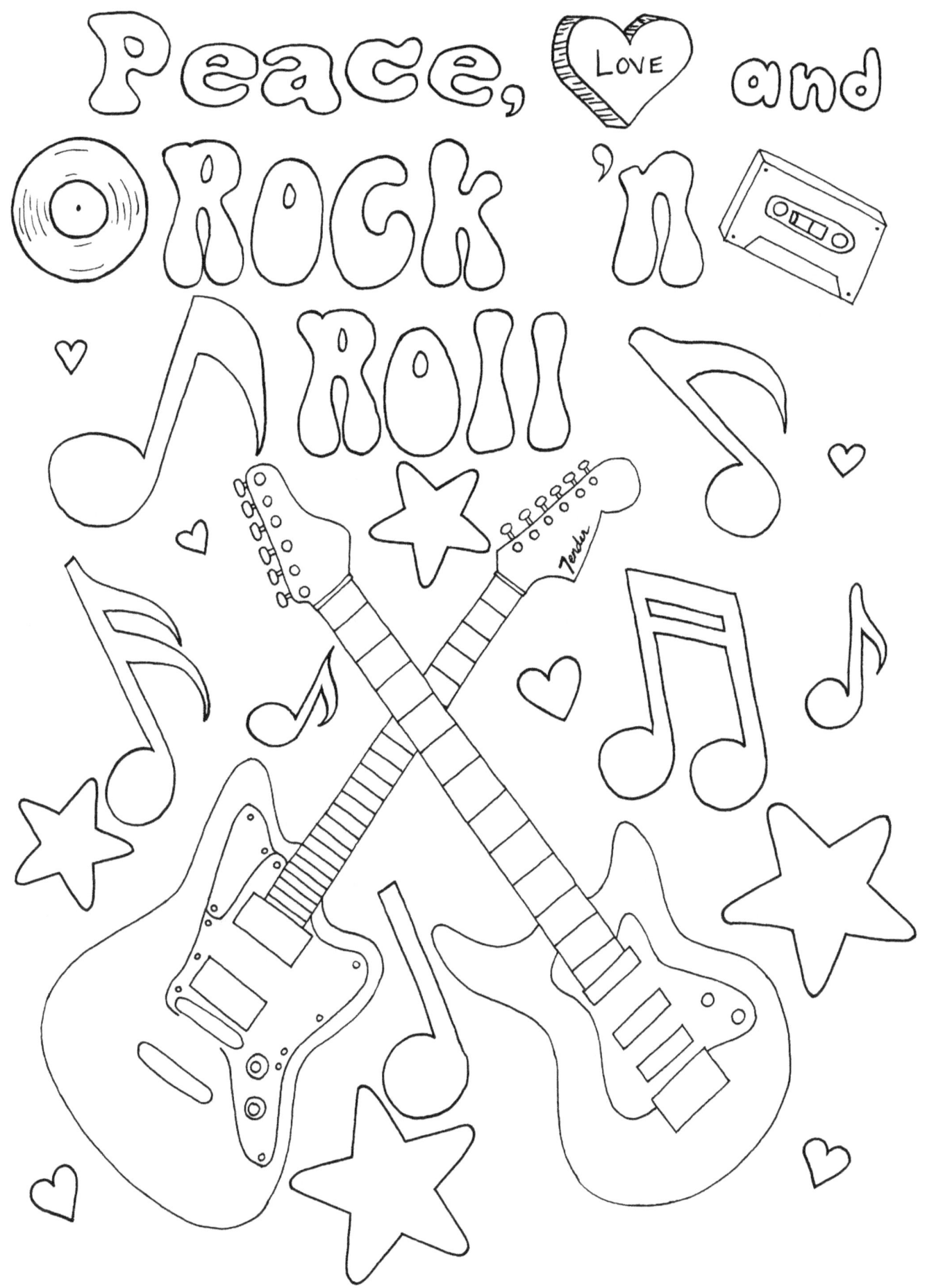

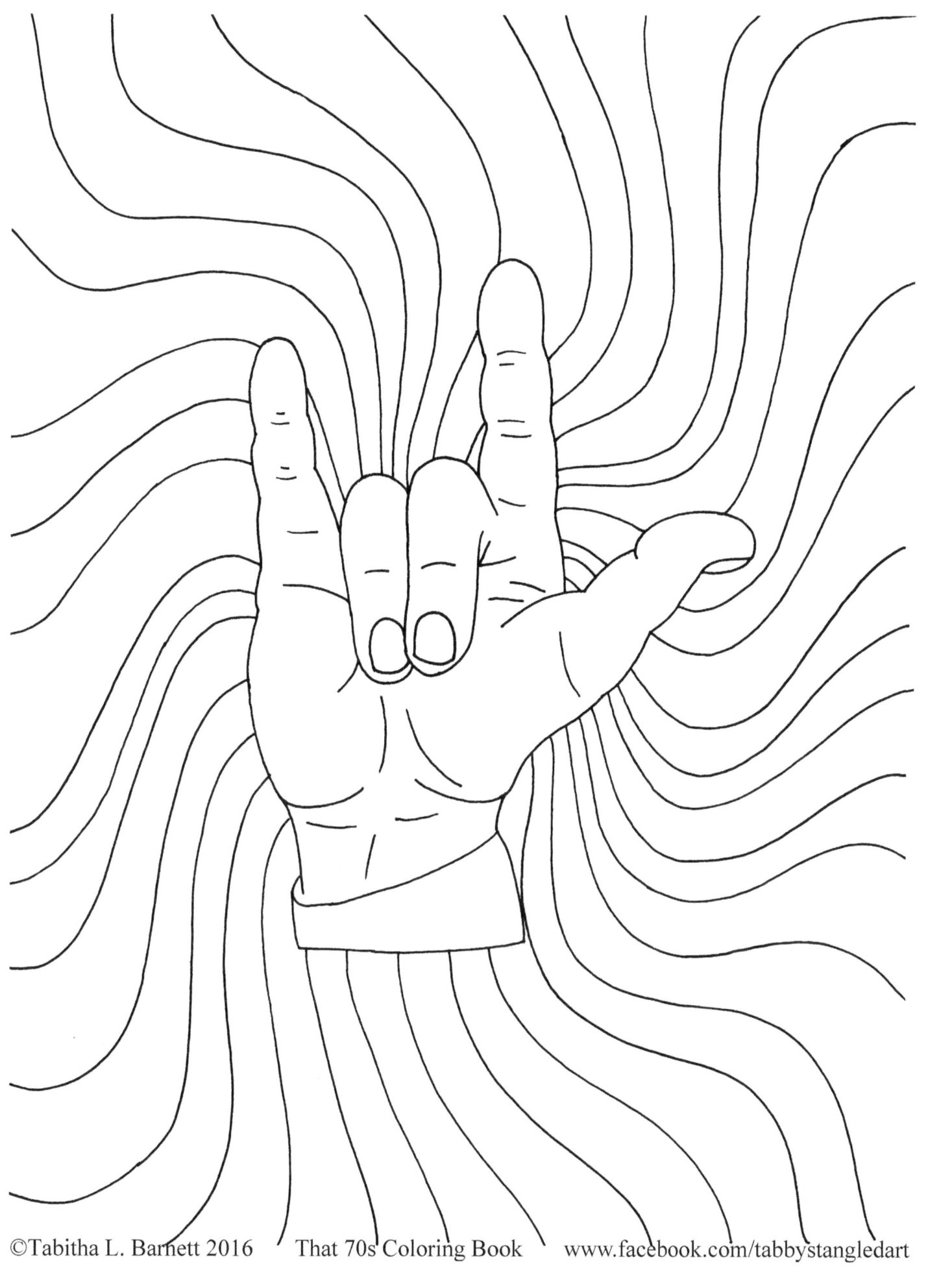

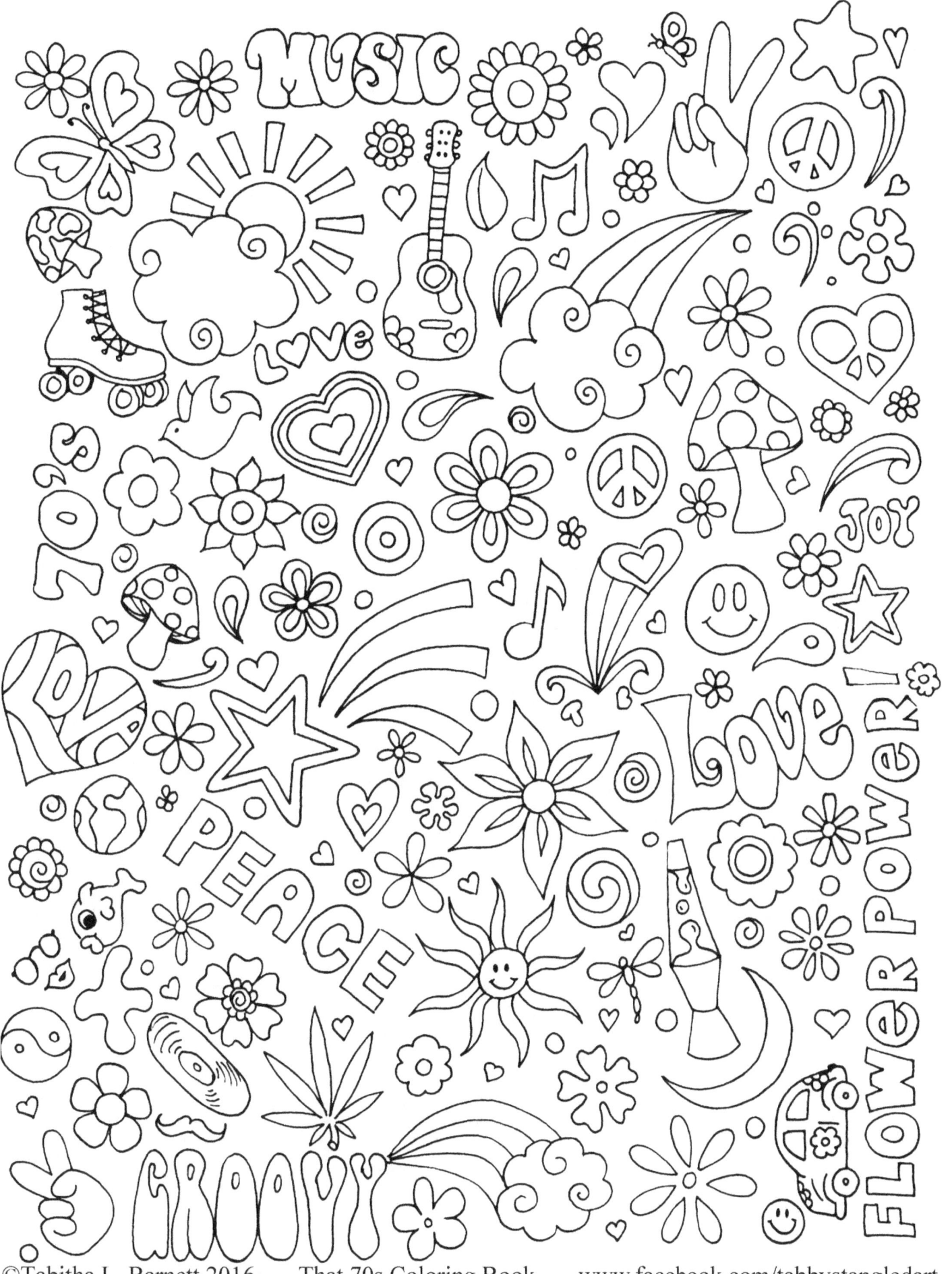

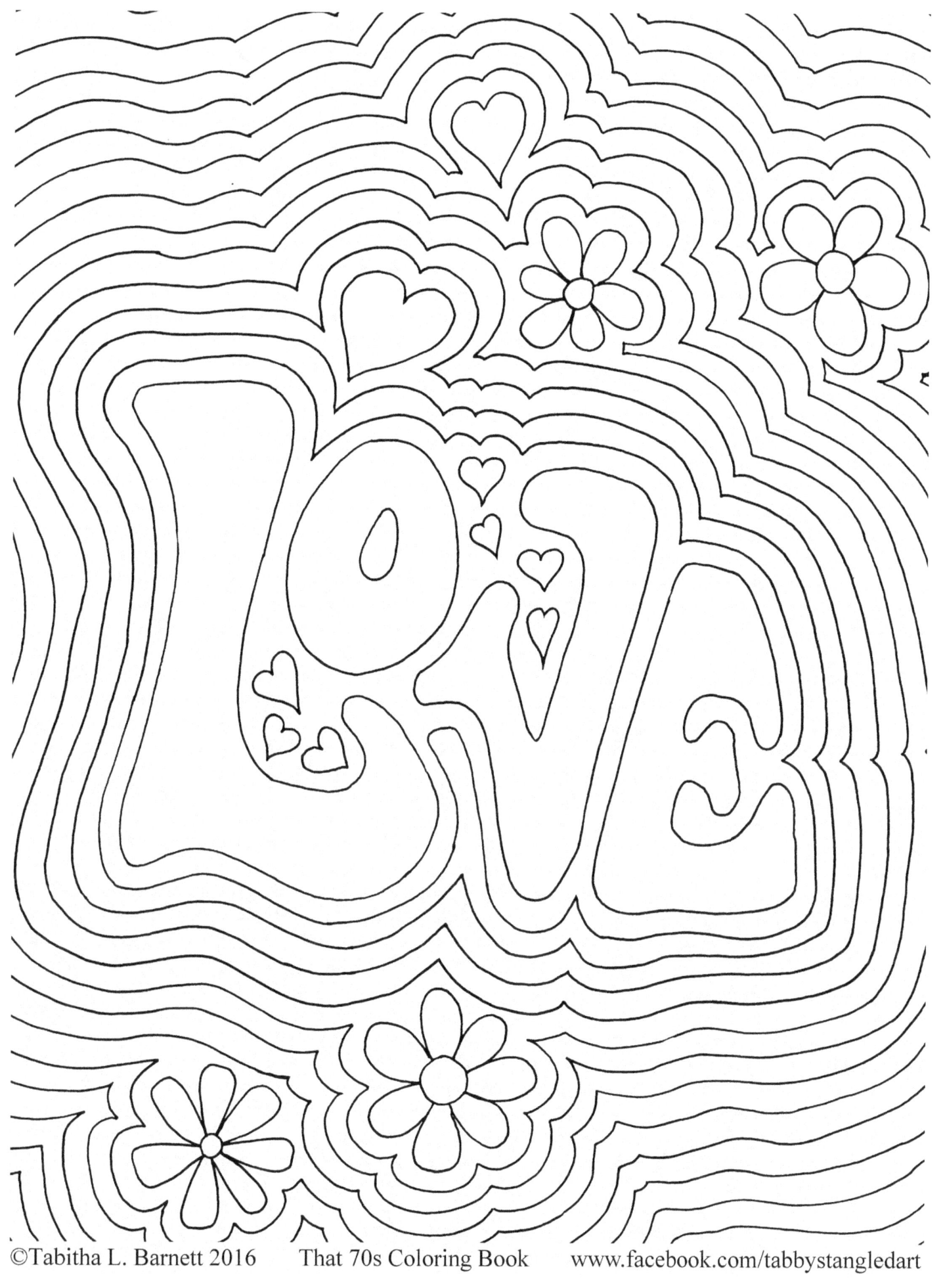

©Tabitha L. Barnett 2016   That 70s Coloring Book   www.facebook.com/tabbystangledart

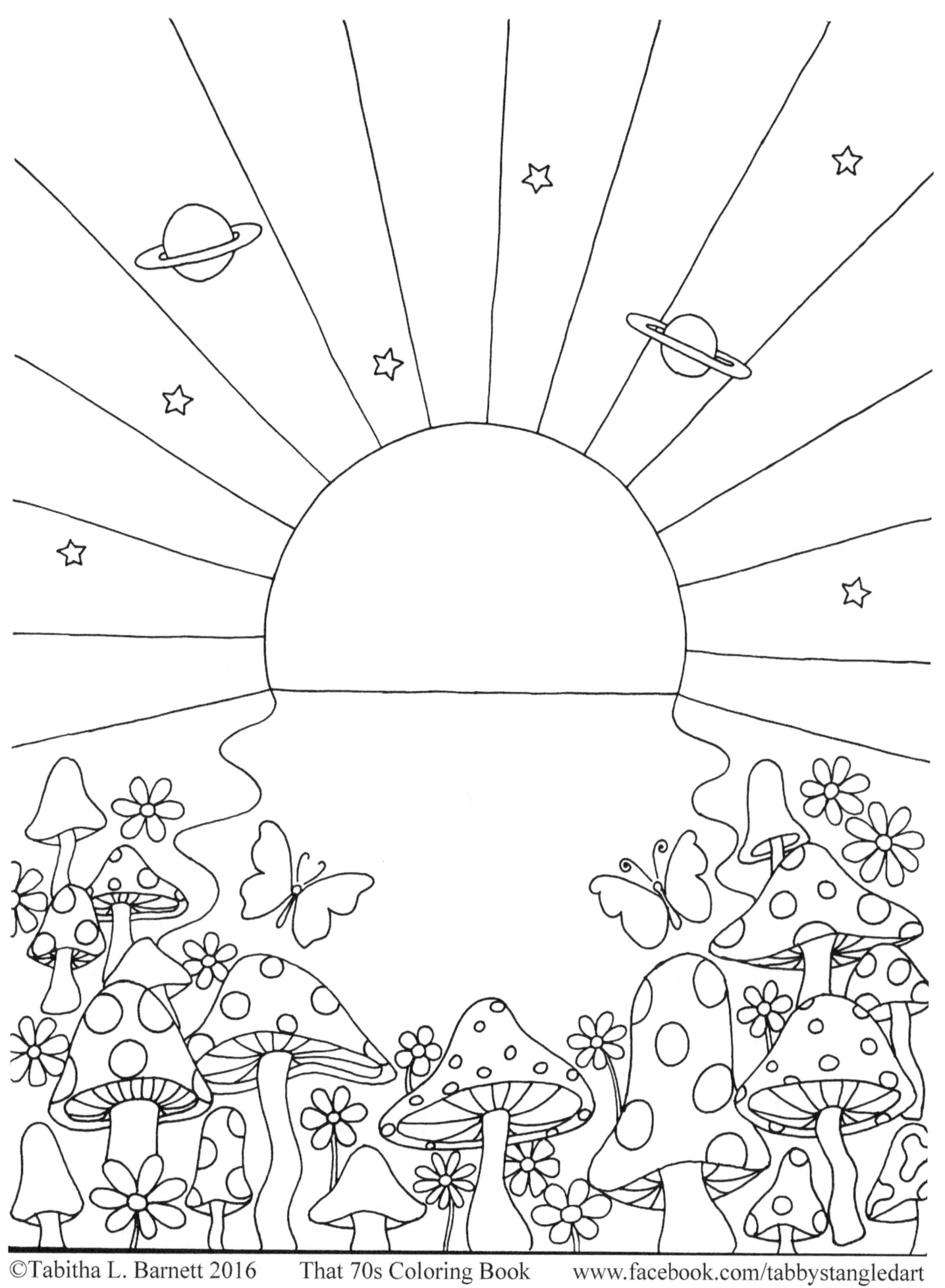

That 70s Coloring Book

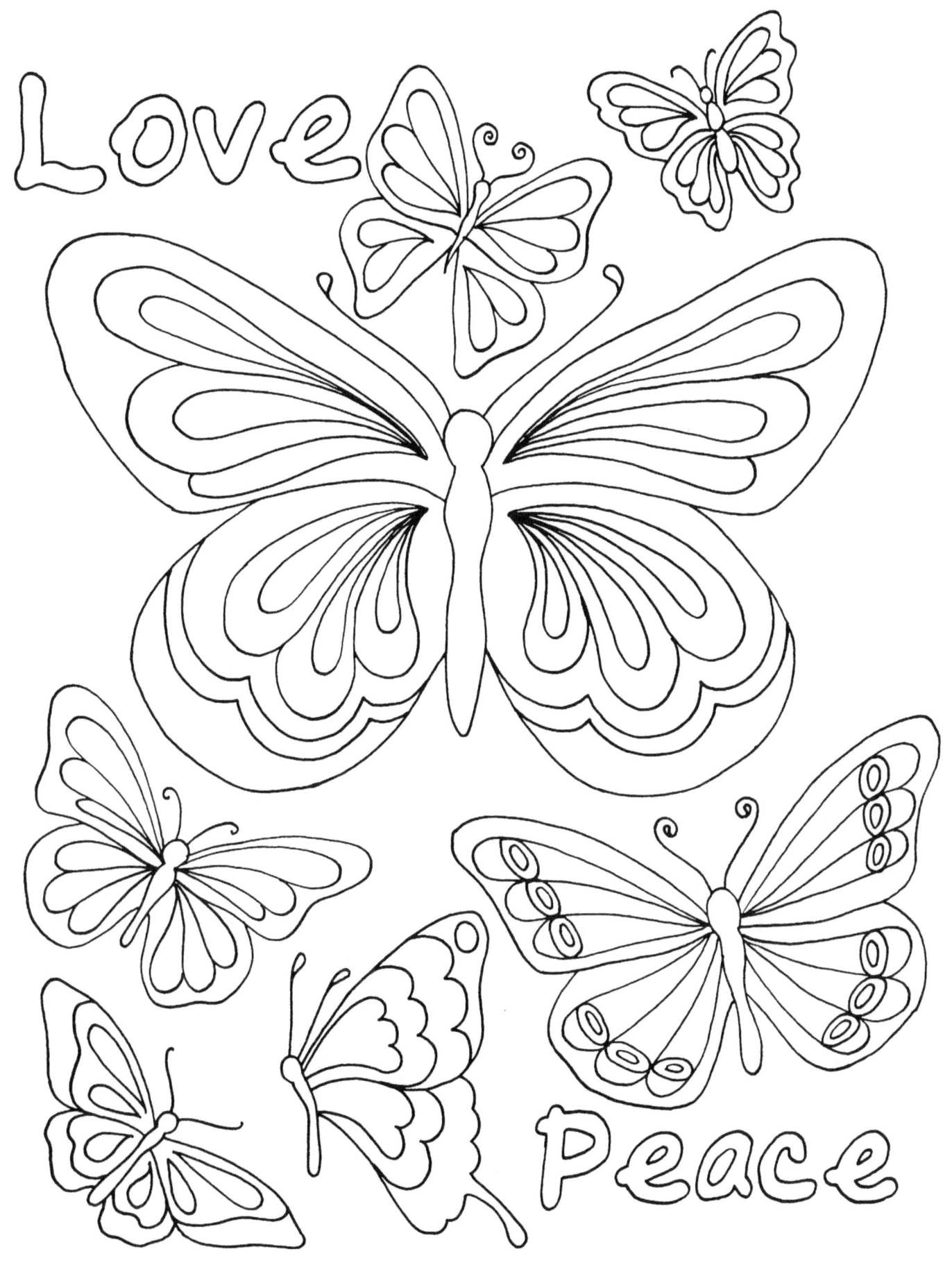

Love

Peace

Thank You for purchasing this book! It was a complete pleasure to create, and I hope you enjoy it as much as I have. I learned so much and discovered so many artists from the era while researching for this book. Some of the pieces were inspired by artwork from the 70s, posters, album covers, and patterns in clothing. Although I wasn't born until '79, I've always LOVED the music of the 70s, and I'm certain I should have been born a decade earlier.

I'd like to take a moment to thank each and every one of you who purchase my books. The Adult Coloring Community has changed my life for the better, and welcomed me with open arms. Not only have I been able to actually do what I enjoy and be home with my family while I "work", but I've also made a great deal of true friends along the way.

If you'd like to learn more about me, my artwork, or my coloring books and pages, check out Tabby's Tangled Art on the web.

Www.facebook.com/tabbystangledart
www.facebook.com/tabby.barnett
Twitter: @tabbyleann
Amazon: http://www.amazon.com/-/e/B015VDR2VA
www.etsy.com/shop/tabbystangledart
www.redbubble.com/people/tabbyb

These extra pages are included to test colors, make notes, create color charts or remove with a ruler and exacto knife to use behind pages to protect from bleeding when using wet mediums.